What Others Are Saying . . .

"In Amos 9:13, Dr. Tim Hill finds a message of urgency and promise for today's church. Refusing to join the doom-sayers who forecast the demise of the church, Dr. Hill sees the Amos 9:13 season as a period of increased opportunity for the church to be part of a last-days movement during which 'the plowman shall overtake the reaper, and the treader of grapes him who sows seed.' Blessings will come in such measure that 'the mountains shall drip with sweet wine, and all the hills shall flow with it.' *The Amos Paradigm—Life at the Speed of Favor*, written in Dr. Hill's inimitable style, needs to be on every Christian's must-read list."

—Dr. Mark L. Williams
General Overseer
Church of God, Cleveland, Tennessee

"Tim Hill is a great preacher . . . and a great writer . . . of both songs and books. In *The Amos Paradigm—Life at the Speed of Favor*, he hits all the right notes. It's his best work ever."

—Dr. Raymond Culpepper
Administrative Bishop
Alabama Church of God
Former Presiding Bishop

"Amos 3:7 tells us that God first reveals his secrets to His prophets. Tim Hill has heard the voice of God giving us hope that we can walk in His favor. In the midst of all the gloom and doom, *The Amos Paradigm—Life at the Speed of Favor* lifts our heads, gives us hope, and leaves us with anticipation. Get ready for it."

—Dr. G. Dennis McGuire
Former General Overseer
Church of God

D0968130

"Tim Hill is a singer, songwriter, and gospel preacher. He has masterfully brought these talents together on this new book. This book will evoke encouragement, challenge, dreams, hope, and repentance. I know Tim Hill, and I know this book was tested in the fires of study, prayer, and deep reflection."

—Lamar Vest
Former President
American Bible Society

"Tim Hill writes from a wealth of experience as an evangelist, pastor, administrative leader, and executive bishop. This book goes the second mile in presenting experiential insight that enriches the meaning of its theme."

—Paul L. Walker
Pastor Emeritus, Mt. Paran Church of God
Atlanta, Georgia

"Dr. Tim Hill is a 'multipurposed' individual. His book, *Beyond the Mist,* thrilled my heart because we need revival for survival. Now, receive this new gift of Tim Hill's writing and be filled with faith that moves the hand of God in the Amos 9:13 season."

—Marcus Lamb
Founder,
Daystar Television Network
Dallas, Texas

"Dr. Tim Hill's new book, *The Amos Paradigm,* will inspire you to seek out a deeper relationship and walk in greater favor than you have ever known. This book will give you the foundational principles you will need to live and move at the 'speed of God's favor.'"

—Garth Coonce
President, TCT Network
Marion, Illinois

"In *Beyond the Mist—A Quest for Authentic Revival*, Tim Hill addressed some keys as to why the United States needs authentic revival. His writings address the hunger growing in the hearts of people seeking after God. *The Amos Paradigm* continues that trend."

—Gordon Robertson
CEO, Christian Broadcasting Network

"Tim Hill shares a profound message from a rather obscure scripture—Amos 9:13, which speaks to the magnitude of God's blessings beyond normal consciousness. In the natural world, nothing travels faster than the speed of light. However, in the spiritual realm, God's divine favor impacts life with speed that supersedes all natural laws and human comprehension. *The Amos Paradigm* presents a divinely inspired and relevant exposition articulating how someone during their Amos 9:13 season can experience overflowing, supernatural, spiritual blessings faster than light or even a nanosecond. This scriptural model will open eyes to a dimension of 'life at the speed of favor.' Definitely a must read!"

—Dr. Michael L. Baker
Administrative Bishop
Church of God, North Georgia

"For more than 35 years, Tim Hill has led many into a deeper experience with God. Spiritual lethargy is his enemy, and it comes through in this book."

—Perry Stone
Founder and President, Voice of Evangelism

"My longtime friend, Bishop Tim Hill, has raised the righteousness bar with this book. He reminds us that God will exceed what we expect, increase what we invest, with the resulting impact of growing God's kingdom. His buoyant optimism and strong faith shine through on every page of this book."

—Dr. Stan Toler
Bestselling author and speaker
Oklahoma City, Oklahoma

"Dr. Tim Hill has brought a biblical balance to the message of faith, prosperity, and favor. The first time he brought this message was at River of Life Assembly of God. Our church knew that we had just heard and witnessed a word from the Lord."

—Dr. Johnny Minick
Pastor, River of Life
Smyrna, Tennessee

"When Dr. Tim Hill brought this message to the Princeton Pike Church, there was a compelling confirmation from the Holy Spirit. A new and thrilling season of favor is here."

—Barry Clardy
Lead Pastor
Princeton Pike Church of God
Hamilton, Ohio

"This is a 'must-read' book. Dr. Tim Hill has been given a fresh word, and favor is coming to the people of God. Having known Tim Hill all my life, I've been influenced by his writing and preaching before, but I'm convinced that God has spoken a life-changing and focused word of revelation through him for these times."

—Pastor Chris Moody
South Cleveland Church of God
Cleveland, Tennessee

"Tim Hill, like David of old, is a gifted preacher/poet. His gift in using the English language is extraordinary. What a joy to pick up this choice volume and have my soul ignited by the spark of truth."

—Pastor Ron Phillips
Abba's House
Chattanooga, Tennessee

The AMOS PARADIGM

Other Titles From Tim Hill

Sermons for Shepherds (Volumes 1-5)

Beyond the Mist: A Quest for Authentic Revival

Heart Songs: A Devotional Journal for Women
by Paula Hill

These books are available from

Tim Hill Ministries
PO Box 8016
Cleveland, TN 37320-8016

The AMOS PARADIGM

Life at the Speed of Favor

TIM HILL

TIM HILL
MINISTRIES
Cleveland, Tennessee

Copyright © 2014 by Tim Hill Ministries

All rights reserved. No portion of this book may be reproduced, stored in a retrieval system, or transmitted in any form or by any means—electronic, mechanical, photocopy, recording, scanning, or other—except for brief quotations in critical reviews or articles, without the prior written permission of the copyright holder.

Printed in Cleveland, Tennessee, by Pathway Press.

Unless otherwise noted, Scripture quotations are taken from the *New King James Version.* Copyright © 1982 by Thomas Nelson, Inc. Used by permission. All rights reserved.

Scripture quotations marked KJV are taken from the King James Version.

Scripture quotations marked NIV are taken from the *Holy Bible, New International Version, NIV,* Copyright © 1973, 1978, 1984, 2011 by Biblica, Inc. Used by permission of Zondervan. All rights reserved worldwide. www.zondervan.com

Scripture quotations marked MSG are from *The Message* by Eugene H. Peterson. © 1993, 1994, 1995, 1996, 2000. Used by permission of Nav-Press Publishing Group. All rights reserved.

Scripture quotations marked NASB are from the *New American Standard Bible,* © Copyright 1960, 1962, 1963, 1968, 1971, 1972, 1973, 1975, 1977 by The Lockman Foundation. Used by permission.

ISBN: 978-1-59684-809-2

Second Printing

Printed in the United States of America

DEDICATION

The Church of God is a Pentecostal denomination rich in history and heritage. From its humble birth in 1886 to becoming a movement of global influence, the Church has nurtured many spiritual sons and daughters. I am one of those sons.

When I was 17 years old, the Church of God embraced me as a minister of the gospel of Jesus Christ and provided a platform that launched a thousand dreams that have been fulfilled again and again. The Church of God brought the gospel to my father, who in turn taught me to honor its biblical doctrines and adhere to its foundational principles for living. I have found friendship with many wonderful and admired church denominations and fellowships around the world, but when I think of home, my heart returns to the Church of God—its songs and sermons; its camp meetings and conventions; its altar calls and prayer lines; its fiery evangelists and statesmen-like pastors; its "bigger than life" leaders. But the values I consider most important are its core values of prayer and the proclamation of God's Word in the spirit and power of Pentecost.

Make no mistake . . . we have always walked hand-in-hand but we haven't always seen eye to eye. The church has honored me during my life's journey and at times solemnly corrected my course. The church has been generous with praise and affirmation, but just as generous with caution and warning. I have rejoiced in the church's triumphs and wept in the church's frailties. The church is neither exempt from struggle nor absolved from criticism, but it has been preserved for this—its finest hour.

The church found me as a child, nourished me through my youth, and accompanied me into my maturity. For all of this, I am thankful and gratefully dedicate this book to the Church of God around the world.

CONTENTS

FOREWORD

D r. Tim Hill has been captured by a specific and prophetic word for our time. While some speak and write in generalities, the message and the promises contained in this book, *The Amos Paradigm*, are uniquely targeted to an end-time audience of undeterred believers.

As a church leader, Tim Hill is known for pushing back against mediocrity on all fronts while vigorously pursuing Kingdom excellence. His voice and godly influence has helped to advance the gospel of Jesus around the world. For many years, I've seen Tim Hill stand up to wrong, speak up for right, and hold up under intense pressure. Dr. Hill has been referred to as a statesman, negotiator, mediator, ambassador, and preacher with a prophetic voice and message. The latter is evident as Dr. Hill unveils the message, tenets, and principles of what he defines as "The Amos Paradigm." The word "remarkable" doesn't begin to describe what lies ahead for all who believe.

Just think of it:

God will exceed all you expect.

The Lord will increase all you invest.

He will accelerate time to accomplish His kingdom purpose in your life.

I believe that God has brought the body of Christ to

this paradigm of living. As Dr. Hill shares in this book, it is more than a season—it's a way of life.

Welcome it.

Embrace it and claim it as your own.

The Amos Paradigm—its time has come.

—Jentezen Franklin
Pastor, Free Chapel Worship Center
Gainesville, Georgia

ACKNOWLEDGMENTS

Any published work is the culmination of numerous forces and influences brought together to produce the finished product.

I gratefully acknowledge the assistance of Dr. Bill George, Janet Price, Toika Sherlin, and Melinda Maness, who assisted in editing and proofing the manuscript; Dr. Tom George, who assisted in the final editing of the book, designed its pages, and coordinated its production; Nellie Keasling, who copyedited the manuscript; and Lonzo T. Kirkland, who designed the cover.

And, I must not fail to acknowledge the inward influence of the Holy Spirit, who daily prompts me to live at the speed of God's favor in this remarkable Amos 9:13 season.

Introduction

The Dawning of the Amos Paradigm

"I'm bringing you into your Amos 9:13 season." Those words couldn't have been more pronounced had I heard them audibly spoken. Hearing them in my spirit, I was awakened early in the morning and immediately reached for my Bible. I had no idea what was written in Amos 9:13.

Still drowsy and with bleary eyes, I began to read: "Behold, the days come, saith the Lord, that the plowman shall overtake the reaper, and the treader of grapes him that soweth seed; and the mountains shall drop sweet wine, and all the hills shall melt" (Amos 9:13 KJV).

After reading the passage from the Old Testament, I said aloud, "Thanks . . . I suppose."

Then I placed the Bible aside, fluffed my pillow, and tried to return to sleep. However, those words would not leave me. As a matter of fact, they continued to rush into my spirit until I was compelled to make my way downstairs and into the study. Once there, I looked toward my bookshelves and reached for *The Message Bible*. I have often gained insight and inspiration from this interpretation of God's Word, and I wanted to see how it rendered Amos 9:13. I was incredibly energized by what I read. The following passage is what I saw:

"Yes indeed, it won't be long now." God's Decree. "Things are going to happen so fast your head will swim, one thing fast on the heels of the other. You won't be able to keep up. Everything will be happening at once—and everywhere you look, blessings! Blessings like wine pouring off the mountains and hills."

As I absorbed that Old Testament passage, I became aware that the Holy Spirit was leading me into a redefined paradigm of living, accentuated by three promises I heard spoken into my spirit.

"I will exceed all you expect."

"I will increase all you invest."

"I will accelerate time to accomplish My kingdom purpose through your life."

What I felt then was beyond mere emotional fervor. I experienced a "faith resurrection." Suddenly, I was moved into a zone of remarkable trust and confidence in God.

I had not experienced that level of miracle faith in quite some time, even though throughout my ministry I have seen miraculous blessings in every realm of living. Often as a young evangelist, I would spend hours each day in prayer in churches where I conducted revivals. Fasting was a lifestyle. As a result, I witnessed a continual flow of favor and manifested blessings from the Holy Spirit. In the more recent years of denominational administration, I had fought against becoming layered with dependence on policy and practice. My faith in God's sovereignty and abandon to His infinite ability were treasures I was unwilling to relinquish. Thankfully, I had always found grace that sustained me in the occasional tension between the two, but to say it had not left me a little worn and fatigued would be less than truthful.

Leading up to my experience that July morning, I was facing a ministry transition with no way of knowing precisely what it might be. The limitations of denominational

18

tenure had caught up with me, and I had no choice but to change course. All these factors made the promises of Amos 9:13 more meaningful—even though I wouldn't have the complete revelation of this experience for a few more days.

Within a week's time from this experience, I was elected to lead World Missions ministries for the Church of God—a Pentecostal denomination in which I've been ordained for nearly 40 years.

By the admission of some, this was an unusual election, not entirely met with celebration. I was not a missionary with "field" experience. Though well-traveled and connected to some degree, it was well known that my ministry had primarily been "stateside."

Accordingly, I had no story of field experience that earned me the right to be selected to such a place. While I had no need for vindication, validation was another issue, and I needed it quickly. But in the moment I stood to accept the nomination and ultimately the election to the position, I heard the words again, "This is your Amos 9:13 season."

I had been previously scheduled to make the appeal for missions in our General Conference. I had discovered upon my election there was nearly a $250,000 deficit in missionary funding and several missionaries were soon to be informed they must return home. It had been determined that the offering would be designated for strengthening this fund.

Amazingly, a miracle began to take shape with every passing hour. For two days, word spread about the need. Pastors and church leaders began to walk up to me with checks in hand, ranging from $1,000 to $20,000. Nationally known ministries began to call with commitments of up to $50,000 in support of missionaries around the world.

By the time I took the stage to present the challenge and receive an offering, I already had $200,000 in my hand. But then something erupted in my spirit, and I watched as over $700,000 was committed to sustaining missionaries on the field. When the final figure was sent to me, I beheld the total through teary eyes. At that moment, I heard the words again: "This is your Amos 9:13 season."

This was the beginning of the most remarkable season I have known in nearly four decades of ministry. With no exaggeration, I have lived a miracle every day for the last year. Throughout this book, I will tell you how this season has affected my family, my finances, and my faith. More than that, I will tell you about a supernatural wave of favor that is targeted for your life known as the Amos 9:13 season. Most of what you are about to experience will be unique to you. Our experiences will be as varied as our unique backgrounds, but I believe this about the Amos 9:13 season: During this remarkable and incredible time ...

God will exceed all you expect.

He will increase all you invest.

He will accelerate time to accomplish His kingdom purpose in you.

Get ready, because this is indeed the Amos 9:13 season in your life.

—Tim Hill
Director, Church of God World Missions

1

A Man Called Amos

When God determines to speak to a generation, He selects a voice and a language that captivates those who hear it. Amos was one of the strangest figures in the Old Testament. In the middle of the ninth century B.C., he suddenly appeared, seemingly from nowhere, uttering a word totally rejected at the time. Then, just as swiftly, he disappeared back into the deserts of Tekoa.

His message was the kind of unpleasant truth that is easier to deny than accept. It was much later that a remnant of God's people began to take the message of Amos seriously. Interestingly, his message continues to illuminate the human situation. The words of Amos are like timed-release capsules that continue to disperse their healing medicine long after they are taken. At the time he said them, they appeared to accomplish nothing, and he was angrily ordered out of Bethel and told to go back to herding his sheep. However, years later, the truth of what he said became apparent, and his message proved to be a crucial factor in helping Israel understand God's covenant and what He wanted from His covenant people.

Amos possessed none of the credentials one would expect for this kind of task and resulting accomplishments. He was actually a desert shepherd and one who tended fig trees. He didn't belong to a family of prominence nor to a circle of the "power elite" in Judah. He came from Tekoa, a desolate region south of Bethlehem near the Dead Sea, which even to this day is virtually uninhabitable.

Although Amos lacked conventional credentials, he did have two distinct advantages that shaped him for this unique ministry.

One was the fact that he and his family had lived in virtual isolation from the rest of Palestine during the five centuries Israel had been there. This meant they had not been contaminated by contacts with pagan religion. The covenant established by God at Sinai still burned in the hearts and minds of these simple folk.

Two, Amos had eyes that were unusually observant. With so little to see or hear in the desert, a shepherd learned to make note of every movement and every sound. His acute power of perception was one of Amos's most notable qualities. Coming into Bethel, he didn't miss a single detail. He took it all in.

This herdsman saw rampant inhumanity as the poor were being exploited. A man could be sold into slavery for just a pair of sandals.

Amos also observed the lavish extravagance of the rich—lying around on couches of ivory, inlaid with gold. He witnessed them drinking wine, not by the glass, but by the bowlful. Amos acknowledged some of the people had grown large from their unbridled indulgence and referred to them as the "cows of Bashan." He was greatly perplexed that many would eat to the point of gluttony while the poor went without any food at all. Injustice was prevalent because the judges could be bought with a few shekels of silver. No one seemed concerned about their fellow man.

When Amos couldn't contain himself any longer, he began to speak with a fresh, but stern word from God. Standing tall with a voice that must have sounded like the roar of a lion, Amos declared two things that startled everyone.

First, Amos told Israel they were ripe for destruction. To illustrate his point, he utilized an interesting visual image of God standing in their midst with a plumb line to determine the state of their soundness, and discovering that nothing about them was secure enough to last. Amos also referred to them as a bowl of over-ripened fruit ready to be thrown out.

Mind you, this was not the gloomy prediction of a chronic doomsayer. This was a shining example of foresight growing out of insight. Looking deeply into the realities of the present, he boldly announced to Bethel: "You have no future bound in your present condition."

The second and extremely insightful proclamation Amos brought forward was as revealing as the first. Elaborating on their bleak future, he gave them the reason behind it. Simply put, they had forgotten their past. Beneath their social problems lay a corrosive soul cancer. When given the opportunity to have a covenant relationship with the one true God, over time, they chose to revert to religious ritual and manmade ceremony that at times even incorporated idol worship.

God wanted a people who would keep covenant with Him, but in keeping covenant, they would also keep relationship.

This explains why Amos stood in the temple in Bethel and declared in the name of God, "I hate and despise your feasts and take no delight in your solemn assemblies. You may offer me your burnt offerings and grain offerings, but I will not accept them" (paraphrase). He went further to declare that their offerings of fattened beasts would not be looked upon nor would they be accepted.

Look carefully at these strong words.

"Take away from Me the noise of your songs; I will not even listen to the sound of your harps. But let justice roll down like waters and righteousness like an ever-flowing stream" (Amos 5:23-24 NASB).

Notice this question, "Did you bring me sacrifices and offerings for the 40 years you were in the wilderness?" (v. 25).

Obviously, the answer was "no."

God wasn't after their rituals and sacrifices. Again, He wanted relationship.

The writings and warnings of Amos are extremely strong and leave one reeling with conviction.

Every chapter is a proverbial trip to the old "woodshed." But like any father, sensitive to his child's needs and driven by a love that is longsuffering, God wouldn't let Amos stop preaching until he offered Israel another chance. With Israel's return to relationship would come an incredible season of promise and prosperity.

A season without struggle and a time of unparalleled harvest—God was longing for an opportunity to show them His elaborate love and unexcelled favor.

Throughout Scripture, various kinds of seasons are described: seasons of grace; seasons of jubilee and restoration; even seasons of repentance. But this particular season would be enormously different, because it would test the very laws of nature. It would challenge the imagination of men and women. This season would energize the faith of the most experienced intercessor.

It would be the Amos 9:13 season.

2

The Already Factor

n "Accelerated Season of Favor" is the best description that can be given of Amos 9:13. It is God's promise that the grueling process of labor will be so compressed that the planted seed will become closer to the gathered harvest. The long span of time usually lodged between your sowing and reaping will become subject to the fast-paced timing of God's intervention in your life. It's the very least that can be expected.

The promise of Amos 9:13 offers a new paradigm of faith and expectation, where old disappointments give way to new realities of expedience and abundant fruitfulness. The old paradigm of religiosity and "system" dependence isn't sustainable anymore. The old paradigms of "doing church" aren't sustainable either. We have arrived at a time when the sludge-like flow of ecclesiastical progress some mistake for Kingdom expansion cannot be tolerated. The harvest demands more from us than that mind-set will ever allow. Today's frequently embraced paradigm and language of "political correctness" dilutes preaching down to a distasteful Pablum, ministry to an ineffective placebo, and will ultimately produce an anemic church. The Amos 9:13 season, however, will be accompanied by prophetic voices whose message will intimidate spiritual darkness and push back against encroaching moral compromise. So rather than "doing church," we begin to "be" the church of the Lord Jesus in the earth today.

Be listening for the voices of those crying in the wilderness saying, "Prepare ye the way of the Lord." Be on the lookout for firebrand preachers who are given more to self-sacrifice than self-preservation. A generation of determined young people is accepting the call to world-changing ministry, and in anticipation of it, they are giving themselves to the "backside of the desert" preparation. If a burning bush of revival happens to ignite while they are there, they'll remove their sandals of worldly dependence and—like Moses—stand on the holy ground of God's sovereignty. With Jehovah on their side, they will lead nations into the promised land of unprecedented harvest.

Indeed, that's the least we can expect ... and it won't be the first time. It's happened before.

Scripture verifies that though the season of plowing and sowing can be grievously long, once the atmosphere is charged with the presence of God's favor, results come quickly.

THE ALREADY FACTOR

Just as God took Moses to the mountain peaks in order to view the Promised Land, you will soon be ascending to spiritual peaks of a divine vantage point. Once there, you will be captured by vision—vision that will mark the rest of your life and introduce you to what is known as God's "already" factor.

Return with me to that conversation Jesus had with His

disciples at Jacob's well. The disciples were pondering how Jesus had introduced "Kingdom living" to a Samaritan woman and, as a result, affected the entire town and ultimately the race with which she was identified. With one statement, Jesus uncovered one of the most dynamic and motivating secrets of reaping a great harvest. He introduced the disciples to the concept of the "already" factor.

In John 4:35, Jesus said, "Say not four months and then comes harvest. Lift up your eyes and behold, the fields are white 'already' unto harvest" (paraphrase).

The word "already" indicated an unusual season of reaping was upon them, a time previously described in Amos 9:13 when the toe of the reaper was on the heel of the planter. They had come to a day of expedient and accelerated breakthrough. The harvest field of souls was no longer considered to be rocky and fallow ground. In the Spirit, they had arrived at a time when instantly thrusting in the "sickle" would bring the harvest. The harvest was "already" available and ripe for gathering.

What a word for you as you read this. God is bringing the already factor into effect in your life and family. Everything you need is already resident within your relationship with the Heavenly Father. Paul said in Ephesians 1:3, "Blessed be the God and Father of our Lord Jesus Christ, who has blessed us with every spiritual blessing in heavenly places in Christ."

What do you need today?

It's already provided.

How do you explain Abraham finding a ram in the brush just before he could sacrifice Isaac? It was the "already" factor (Genesis 22:11-14).

What accounts for the coin Peter found in the mouth of the fish at tax-paying time? It was the "already" factor (Matthew 17:24-27).

It was the "already" factor that Elisha's servant finally discovered when his spiritual eyes were opened in Dothan one day. Once spiritual perception took over, he saw the angels of God had "already" surrounded the enemy. Scripture declares the "angel of the Lord encamps about those who fear Him" (Psalm 34:7).

The angels are "already" there.

Your provision is "already" there.

Your victory is "already" there.

In the Amos 9:13 season of living, your anxiety will give way to the confidence that comes with seeing what is already yours through Christ Jesus.

Some time ago while reading through the Bible, I came upon what seemed to be the endless genealogies of the patriarchs found in the pages of the Old Testament. Reading in Exodus 1:5, I was reminded of the sons of Jacob who went into Egypt with him during the time of famine. Starting with Rueben and ending with Asher, a total of 11 sons are listed as being with Jacob when he arrived. However, Jacob was father to 12 sons. The one not listed with the others is Joseph. In your Bible, you will see Joseph's name isolated and standing alone from the others and encased between parenthesis symbols. Within those symbols you will discover a treasure almost hidden away in what some would consider parenthetical insignificance. Here is how it is written in the Bible, complete with the parentheses:

(for Joseph was in Egypt *already*).

The impact of that little phrase is explosive in my spirit. Think about it. The man God would use to sustain his father and brothers was already in place before their arrival. Through Joseph, the foresight and insight needed to guide a country through a famine was already in place before the famine even started. Pharaoh didn't have to import a financial genius from some faraway place in order to secure Egypt's endangered economy. His best economist and financial strategist were already there. The answer was in place before the problem ever manifested.

So it was with the provision for our soul's redemption. Long before sin marred the complexion of humankind, there was a "Lamb slain from the foundation of the world" (Revelation 13:8).

So it is with your life. In this miraculous season of God's favor, you'll discover that His blessings and provision will precede you and enable you to make the difference in others.

In this dynamic season, you will see as never before the reality of 2 Corinthians 9:10: "Now He who supplies seed to the sower and bread for food will also supply and increase your store of seed and will enlarge the harvest of your righteousness" (NIV).

Count on it. It's already there.

3

The Season of Exceeded Expectations

Through the prophet Amos, God verified to His people that without delay, there would be a reaping of an unbounded harvest. Amos further prophesied such an abundant yield of grapes that it would be like a river of wine flowing down from vineyards on the surrounding mountains. This prophecy defied the usual anticipation of farmers and vinedressers. Who would normally expect such things? After years of drought and depression, Israel had come to expect very little.

An epidemic of global proportions exists today. It transcends boundaries, cultures, and languages. It's an epidemic of pessimism and dead expectations. Far too many people are suffering from an expired "expect-er." As a result, many have more faith in failure than they have hope in victorious living.

A God of miracles seems foreign to many sitting on church pews today. Attending some churches in today's negative atmosphere is to be subjected to an hour of listless worship spawned by lifeless choral dirges and unconvincing sermons. Where is the expectation that David seemed to have when he said, "I was glad when they said unto me, 'Let us go into the house of the Lord'" (Psalm 122:1)?

Where is the anticipation that seems to come through in his words of Psalm 100:4 when he sang: "Enter into His gates with thanksgiving, and into His courts with praise. Be thankful to Him, and bless His name"?

I wonder, could a good trip to church evoke such anticipation now? Our level of expectation has everything to do with what we receive or do not receive from God.

When Peter and John went to the Temple to pray, they came upon a crippled man whom they possibly had seen before. He had been in this condition from birth, and his daily routine involved having his family or friends carry him to a place called the Beautiful Gate, just outside the Temple proper. There, this pitiful man would beg for money and food. I wonder how many had passed by him on a daily basis and could never help him? No one expected that a difference could ever be made in his condition. Similarly, the cripple never expected that anyone could help him obtain a better life.

There were many things wrong with this man besides his crippled condition. Let me list a few.

THE BEGGAR'S LABEL

He had a name, I suppose, but we're not told what it was, and I doubt if many knew it anyhow. He was, however, known throughout the community as "The Cripple."

Life's labels can often be more difficult to deal with than life's circumstances. It could be that you have dealt with a label all your life. I'm amazed at how easily we get them, but even more amazed at the damage they can do. Maybe you acquired your first label in grade school when you received your first report card. It couldn't be missed. There it was, emblazoned in the big black letter "F." That little paper card felt as if it weighed two tons as you carried it home to your mom or dad.

As you grew older, life's labels became more complex. Now it's divorce, bankruptcy, moral failure, alcoholism, or maybe a false accusation, and no one chooses to believe your side of the story. Bottom line: It's a label wrapped around your life that people see and read long before they get a chance to know the "real" you.

Like the man at the gate, you have a name, but no one knows it, and furthermore, they choose not to learn it. It's just easier to refer to you as "the cripple."

Let me tell you something about labels. A label is only someone's opinion, and your Heavenly Father feels much differently about you than those who have pinned life's labels to your lapel.

In the Bible, the name "Jacob" meant "worm," but God called him "Prince," when He changed his name to "Israel."

Gideon was a coward hiding from the enemy, but God called him a "mighty man of valor."

The name "Peter," meant "small stone," but Jesus called him "Rock."

Saul was a murderer, chasing down Christians to throw them into jail, but Jesus changed his life and his name. He became Paul, who wrote over half of the New Testament.

I shouldn't confess this here, but I will. As a kid, I was always curious about the labels attached to the pillows that came with the clear warning, "Do Not Remove!" Maybe my attitude was wrong, but I thought, "This is my pillow on my bed. I put my head on it, sleep on it, and dream on it." So, I decided one day I would see what happened if I pulled that label off.

Guess what happened? Absolutely nothing!

The house didn't fall. The pillow didn't come apart nor did it slap me in the middle of the night.

Nothing happened. Absolutely nothing.

I challenge you to rip off the label.

You are not someone's opinion. You are who the righteous and caring God says you are. Rise up in the name He has given you and take hold of your promising future.

THE BEGGAR'S LAMENESS

Common thought infers that the man at the Beautiful Gate had twisted or deformed limbs. Who really knows? He could just as easily had perfectly formed ankles and feet, with no strength or muscular stamina that allowed them to function. Scripture does record that at his moment of healing, "his feet and ankle bones received strength" (Acts 3:7). This could imply the possibility of acceptable form without obvious function. At the end of the day, even if his legs looked normal, he was lame. He was lame in his legs as well as in his life.

Does that describe you?

You look good, but you're lame.

You have the form, but you're weak.

You're going through the motions, but your motions aren't getting you anywhere. You have . . .

- Lame intentions and lame living.
- Lame excuses and lame results.

- Nothing to stand on.
- No foundation to support you.
- So many limits brought on by so much lameness.

You've dragged yourself from one gate to the next, looking for the next "handout," when the real answer lies in a heaven-sent "hand up."

THE BEGGAR'S LIMITS

How much can a lame man do when the limits of crippled existence have been placed upon him?

Life's limits are chains that bind one's soul to frustration and hopelessness. The man at the Beautiful Gate was constrained and contained. He could travel only so far and reach only so high. His future was as bleak as his past.

According to Levitical law, he was not even permitted to go inside the Temple due to his infirm condition (Leviticus 21:17-24). He would always get just as close as possible by sitting at the gate. There, he could possibly hear the music, the prayers, or even the exhortations that came from the priests. Most important, he placed himself in the path of those coming and going to worship, hoping to receive some financial benevolence.

In some respects, he found himself on a leash—mentally, spiritually, and in many regards, physically. The length of his leash put him in sight and hearing distance of his deliverance, but this resulted in limited faith.

RESUSCITATED EXPECTATION

After years of disappointed hopes, he encountered two anointed preachers fresh from a Pentecostal experience in the Upper Room. Coming in contact with their inspired faith, something changed within him.

The Scriptures record in Acts 3:1-8 the entire story, but notice these particular words in verse 5: "And he (the lame man) gave heed unto them, *expecting* to receive something from them" (*italics mine*, KJV).

Expectation had been dead in him for a long time, but the moment he came in contact with inspired faith emanating from others, it blazed to life again.

Has your faith been dormant for so long that now your expectations are completely dead? Allow me to stir up your faith by reminding you that you have access to the awesome power of a providing God who will by far exceed anything you can expect from any other source.

Paul made it plain in Ephesians 3:20 that Jehovah God is "able to do exceeding abundantly above all that we ask or think, according to the power that works within us" (KJV).

The power working within you is Spirit-inspired and expectant faith that believes for all things at all times. You can express it today, and activate the start of your Amos 9:13 season.

Some time ago, I was reminded of the power of expectation when a young man approached me in a conference where I was speaking. His story took me back 20 years.

A young mother, introduced to me by my secretary as Mrs. Evans, walked into my office. She informed me her newborn and premature son was near death in Infant ICU. She held in her hands a small tape recorder and asked to record a prayer as I prayed for her child's healing. Few times had I witnessed such desperate faith.

I prayed for the baby, and the prayer, along with its unction, was captured on the cassette. By special permission of the doctors, she placed the recorded prayer within the incubation crib near the child. I'm sure the physicians thought they were simply pacifying a frantic mother with little hope. Remarkably, the desperate and expectant faith of this young mother reached God, and immediately the child began to respond. I had heard little after the initial report, but as I was standing in the lobby of the convention center in Greensboro, North Carolina, where I was speaking that night, a young United States Marine approached me and said, "My name is Tyler Evans, and I've waited 20 years to meet you." Tyler went on to relate the story of his healing that began when his mother touched an "exceeding and abundant God" who honored her faith. That night, I introduced Tyler to a congregation appreciative of his service to our nation as a Marine. They gave him a standing ovation. But beyond that, they stood to praise the God who responds to expectant faith by hearing and answering prayer.

Tyler's story simply reminds me that this is a powerful season of the miraculous, and God will indeed exceed all we expect.

4

A Heavenly Return on Kingdom Investments

The Amos 9:13 season is about unusual favor and increase. The Bible describes numerous accounts of what I call "grace seasons," when unprecedented favor flowed like rivers upon God's people. It's significant to note that these seasons seem to be tied to the recipients' acts of trust and obedience. The common thread that weaves each occurrence together is the amazing increase and return God gave in response to a "faith investment." The corporate world would liken it to what is known as the "ROI," which stands for "Return on Investment."

Observe the pattern:

• After a series of offerings, Abraham multiplied in riches even while famine was making its mark on Egypt (Genesis 13:1-2).

• Isaac sowed seed in the famine-stricken land of Gerar and received a hundredfold return (Genesis 26:12).

• Jacob built altars and gave offerings and increased in spite of the deceitful tactics of his enemies (Genesis 35:14).

• Joseph employed various practices of investment and sowing and, as a result, Egypt prospered while other nations suffered (Genesis 41:46-57).

I could just as easily write about David, Solomon, and many others described in both Old and New Testament pages, who experienced seasons of favor that exceed all expectations. Allow me, however, to take you to the inspiring account of Jesus feeding the multitude. This story perfectly showcases the wonderful ability of God to greatly increase, by far, more than any of us ever invest.

A CHALLENGE TO FAITH

Imagine it for a moment. Five thousand men are there, along with an undisclosed number of women and children, sitting everywhere. They're tired and hungry, and they all have a long walk home with no food in sight (Matthew 14:14-21).

There is nothing like a good dilemma to test one's faith. That's exactly what Philip faced when confronted with the question Jesus asked: "Where will we buy bread to feed these people?" (see John 6:1-6).

Always remember when Jesus asks a question, it's not because He needs the information. As a matter of fact, Scripture records in John 6:6, "He himself knew what He would do." Jesus was simply testing Philip's faith. Jesus wanted from him what He always desires from us—faith. Instead of exercising faith, Philip gave Jesus what He already had—the facts.

Jesus is never unaware of the facts. Simply put, He knows. He knows the details of your life, as well as your overwhelming concerns. Philip's short answer was, "Lord, No. It just can't be done, and there are three reasons why:

- "There are too many people.
- "There's not enough money.
- "It's too late in the day anyhow."

Sad to say, I still find that attitude here and there as I travel.

You'll see it in some churches, and you'll find it in the hearts of some people. Too much. Too little. Too late.

Suddenly, Andrew stepped up alongside a young child with his basket lunch of two small fish and five small loaves of bread. Just as Andrew was about to take delight in the fact he had found a possible solution, he caught a glimpse of the multitude and then said, "There is a lad here, but on second thought, I'm sorry I brought him, because what is this among so many?" (6:9).

At that very moment, Jesus asked for an investment—an investment of faith primarily, but also an investment of resources. The Savior looked at the child and said, "Son, if you will do just one thing, I can feed this crowd. Transfer what is in your hand into mine."

That was the only instruction then and it's the only instruction now. Just transfer the contents of your hand; but inherent in that command is trust, abandon, confidence, and surrender to the Master. Can you do that?

A FAITH THAT TRANSFORMS

If you can and if you will, here is the result you will receive: God will transform all that you transfer.

Transfer your time into God's hands, and He will transform one hour of labor into years of fruitful results.

Transfer your talent, and God will transform it into a gift that brings you before kings and opens unbelievable doors of opportunity.

Transfer your treasure into your Father's hands, and

He will make accessible to you His divine and eternal storehouses of provision with His commitment to always "supply all your need according to His riches in glory by Christ Jesus (Philippians 4:19).

It all begins with the opening of your hand.

Had the child held tightly to his little lunch, then that's all he would have ever had—a little lunch.

The opening of his hand allowed for the human transfer, and that became the divine transformation.

Look what happened to that investment. Every man, woman, and child was fed. The child's food multiplied as the disciples began to distribute it; so much so, that by day's end, they gathered up 12 baskets of leftovers.

That's what I call "increase."

In this remarkable season, you can expect the blessing of increase.

It will be a time of scriptural fulfillment.

How I long for balance in the message of biblical prosperity today! A doctrinal imbalance concerning any scriptural theme will ultimately lead to abuse and error in the body of Christ. Please understand, contrary to how some may present it, God's promise of "increase" applies as much to sowing mercy, forgiveness, and good deeds as it does money.

Jesus wasn't receiving an offering in Luke 6:38 when He said, "Give and it will be given unto you." While this promise may certainly apply to finances, it actually refers to the currency of forgiveness and our need to be more merciful and less judgmental of one another.

I'm convinced that this is the season of anticipated expansion in these and all other human and spiritual arenas.

For example, according to Isaiah 26:3, God will increase your peace. "You will keep him in perfect peace whose mind is stayed on You."

In Joshua 24:13, God promised to expand favor for your family. "I have given you a land for which you did not labor, and cities which you did not build, and you dwell in them; you eat of the vineyards and olive groves which you did not plant."

Malachi 3:10 promises surplus to those who will be faithful to the Lord in tithing. "Bring all the tithes into the storehouse, that there may be food in My house, and try Me now in this," says the LORD of hosts, "If I will not open for you the windows of heaven

And pour out for you such blessing that there will not be room enough to receive it."

The desire of the Father for you is that you "Enlarge the place of your tent and let them stretch out the curtains of your dwellings. Do not spare; lengthen your cords and strengthen your stakes" (Isaiah 54:2).

Your fruitfulness brings great delight to our Heavenly Father. "Beloved, I wish above all things that you would prosper and be in health, even as your soul prospers " (3 John 1:2).

The Amos 9:13 season will bring increase and expansion for the body of Christ. As we transfer our trust and faith to our Father in heaven, He will wondrously transform all we place in His care.

HOW MUCH DO YOU TRUST ME?

I'm very careful to share the following account, but I do so only to affirm the blessing of divine transfer and transformation.

Entering into my work as a denominational leader in World Evangelization, I was mantled with the daily responsibility of overseeing the financial stabilization and advancement of the denomination's missions and missionary outreach. Let me state clearly and concisely, there was an extremely fruitful ministry of missions before my arrival and there will be after my departure. It doesn't rise and fall upon my presence, and I know that assuredly. With that said, I was met head-on with a quarter of a million dollar deficit in missionary funding and a loan portfolio that was nearly a half-million in deficit per year. In addition, a denominational decision that translated into a "real-dollars" loss of at least $1 million per year had come into effect and was scheduled to continue for most of my tenure. Combined together, these factors contributed to a loss of 50 percent to the basic operational budget of the missions arm of the denomination.

For a specific and special period of time, I became keenly aware of the hovering presence of the Holy Spirit. In prayer one night, I received specific and individual instruction regarding my own commitment and trust related to my personal financial stewardship.

I had wrestled with the dilemma of missionaries being expected to raise their funds in a difficult global economy, along with the rapidly changing approach to missions ministry. I was also struggling with the fact that as CEO of the denomination's missions organization, it seemed that, by necessity, I would be responsible for reducing the staff of long-time, faithful employees who had given many years to missions service. Every day, I was becoming more aware that schools, seminaries, clinics, and orphanages faced closure unless financial miracles became a regular occurrence.

In the midst of these dismal considerations, I heard this question in my spirit, "How much do *you* really trust me?"

I responded with my typical Christian preacher answer. I said, "Lord, I trust you with everything I have."

Immediately, I felt the strongest impression I've ever had in my life. "Then give me a year of it."

I felt God had instructed me to totally relinquish a

year's income from my position as the denomination-al missions leader. Please understand, I'm not remote-ly suggesting anyone should ever do this. There are no heroic benefits to doing such a thing. You will question yourself a thousand times, and a few people you confide in will question your judgment a thousand times more.

My first response was to question all I was feeling. My second response was to test it theologically, philosophi-cally, and emotionally. I even invented a way I thought I could legitimately give God what He was asking for and not necessarily feel any cost. I initially said, "Fine, Lord, I'll raise the equivalent of a year's salary." I soon realized that was not what God had asked me to do. Fund-rais-ing comes with my job, and anyone who holds the posi-tion is expected to be able to accomplish it.

Deep in my heart, I knew that incomplete obedience was really total disobedience. I had to do it, and through a series of unusual events, I came to that final conclusion.

My paycheck had just been laid on my desk. The pa-per it was formatted on was the typical size of any check, but it seemed to cover my entire desk. I stared at it for a long time, contemplating God's direction. In a moment of "now-or-never" faith, I called my financial officer and somewhat tersely said, "Come up to my office—now!"

He walked in, and in his presence I signed the back of the check and said, "Don't bring me another one for 11 more months." He seemed stunned. I said, "Take it and go before I change my mind."

You ever heard of buyer's remorse? I immediately had a bad case of giver's remorse. The room didn't light up and no angels sang. There were no euphoric feelings of grandeur that I had obeyed God.

There was, however, an unusual assurance that re-gardless of how I was feeling emotionally, I had done all I could to obey the Lord's direction.

I was not prepared for what was about to happen. Within a week's time, amazing favor began to manifest everywhere I turned.

Songs I had written years ago were selected by various artists for recording projects. Invitations to a series of interdenominational events began to pour into my office. In every direction I looked, those "make-your-head-swim" blessings were coming at me. Within 10 days, I had restored back to me the entire year's income I had felt impressed to give away!

I realized once again, in a most dramatic way, I had experienced the miracle of the Amos 9:13 season. God had surely increased all I had invested.

I don't relate this testimony to encourage anyone to give away anything more than God ever directs. However, I can, with all assurance, tell you that your Father will never be in debt to you or anyone else. The promise of reaping from what is sown really does come true. When you invest in the Kingdom economics of souls, you will discover your investment is never subject to the tremors of Wall Street or the shutdowns in Washington, DC.

I have paraphrased what Jesus said to Peter in Mark 10:29-30:

> Let me assure you that no one has given up anything: home, brothers, sisters, mother, father, children, or property for love of Me and to tell others the good news, who won't be given back a hundred times over—homes, brothers, sisters, mothers, children, and land; with persecutions—all these will be his here on earth, and in the world to come, he shall have eternal life.

Now that's what I call a great "Return on Investment!"

5

The Speed of Favor

I am convinced that the closer we get to the manifestation of the kingdom of heaven, the less confining seasons will become. I believe we have entered into a prophesied era of Amos 9:13, when typical concepts and understandings of seasons will be eclipsed by the power of God. To grasp that thought, it is important to remember Amos was a shepherd-farmer and God spoke to him in expressions and metaphors that farmers could easily understand. He talked in "harvest" terms when he spoke about the plowman and the reaper—the two major, most important people in the process of sowing and reaping.

The plowman was responsible for preparing the ground for planting, and obviously the reaper was responsible for gathering the harvest from the previously planted seeds. There is, however, in the Amos text, a most unusual description given as it relates to the sequence and timing of their respective labors. The Lord declared that the plowman shall overtake the reaper. The word *overtake* is defined in dictionary terms as "catching up with and even passing by something or someone." The scriptural use of this term strongly indicates a swift and accelerated process of bringing in the harvest so that the distance between seed planting and harvesting becomes shorter and shorter.

A farmer's understanding of the typical planting and harvest process dictates that a time span of four months has to transpire before any reaping can be done. This is established in nature and even verified by Scripture. In Genesis 8:22, after Noah had built an altar to God, a promise was made that farmers have lived and died by ever since: "As long as the earth endures, seedtime and harvest; cold and heat; summer and winter; night and day will never cease" (NIV).

However, Jesus, one day when speaking to His disciples, alluded to a supernatural adjustment that would affect one's typical understanding of harvest time, as recorded in John 4:35. He met the woman from Sychar who came to draw water at Jacob's Well. After a lengthy conversation, Jesus introduced her to living water. The disciples struggled with the new idea of reaping a spiritual Samaritan harvest. They seemed perhaps to be thinking that maybe someday, if given enough time and after working through enough religious traditions, the Samaritans might be reached . . . but surely not now.

Jesus addressed their limited vision with the stern John 4:35 directive: "Do not say any longer, four months and then comes harvest. I say to you, Behold, the fields are white already unto harvest" (paraphrase). The Master was making it crystal clear that their normal understanding of the season—with all of its enormous hindrances and challenges—had been eclipsed by God's supernatural intervention. He declared to them, "Harvest is now!"

Even the established order of nature is no match for God's divine and hastened interruptions.

The established order of religion is no match for God's miracle timing, either. The Lord's visit to the synagogue is recorded in Luke 4. Jesus entered there one day and sat among many who were looking for the Messiah— but not that day and not Him. After all, He was the poor son of a poor carpenter. Besides, they thought the Messiah with all of His promises and hopes for a New Israel surely couldn't come for another 1,000 or 2,000 years.

Jesus was invited to read from the sacred scrolls the passage from Isaiah 61:1-2. He began reading with clarity and anointing the prophetic words foretelling the coming of Messiah. "The spirit of the Lord is upon me because he has anointed me to preach the gospel to the poor; he hath sent me to heal the brokenhearted, to preach deliverance to the captives, and recovering of sight to the blind, to set at liberty them that are bruised, [and] to preach the acceptable year of the Lord" (KJV). After reading, Jesus took His seat and while everyone was waiting for the synagogue elders to comment, Jesus spoke up without hesitancy or awkwardness, saying, "This day is this scripture fulfilled in your ears" (KJV). His hearers were shocked to hear Jesus say such a thing, but perhaps more astounded at the thought that Almighty God had suddenly accelerated time in their very presence, annihilated their calendars, put their timepieces into hyperspeed, and brought the Year of Jubilee right into the middle of their day!

What are time and seasons to God anyway? He sits above the circle of the earth, says Job. Below, time has a beginning and an end, but He is above it all. He moves in and out of time at His pleasure, and years become months, and months become weeks. Weeks become days, and days become minutes. Minutes become seconds, and seconds transform into instantaneous miracles of God's manifested glory.

WHAT IS SEEDTIME?

Seedtime refers to more than a specific moment, day, or month. Some Bible teachers interestingly interpret Genesis 8:22 by actually separating the word, "seedtime" into "seed" and "time" to indicate that an undesignated length of time is involved in the process. Their interpretation of Genesis 8:22 is understood in this manner: "As long as the earth remains, there will be seed, time, and harvest." Again, the idea is highlighted that time comes between planting and reaping. There is a season of planting and then a season for reaping and a whole lot of working, watering, weeding, and waiting in between.

Allow me to break down the typical season for you. Every season that led to a great harvest usually involved four things: (1) Working, (2) Watering, (3) Weeding, and (4) Waiting.

WORKING

With this established season comes the expectation that three to four months of labor and toil must be endured as well. Since the days of Adam, no one expects anything less than the "sweat of your face" (Genesis 3:19). There's never a harvest without months of hard work. We dig and plow and then plow some more. It seems like a never-ending cycle of labor that leaves us with calloused hands, aching backs, and sore muscles as we prepare to sow for a future harvest.

Of course, God was speaking to Adam about hard and fallow ground when He implied plowing would result in excruciating weariness. And to think, all this hard toil because the ground had come under the curse of sin brought about by Adam's fall. It's hard to imagine how life might have been before man's transgression made it so difficult.

When Amos wrote of plowing, he was familiar with the common practice of his time. Late October was typically the time of preparing the ground, left hard from the searing heat of summer, but now softening with the biblical "early rain." A single wooden stake with an iron tip was normally used; it was usually pulled by a pair of oxen or donkeys. The animals were yoked together. An ox goad, a long staff with a nail or metal tip, was used to control the animals. The plowman had the double duty of applying pressure to keep the plow deep enough into the dirt to turn the soil while controlling the often contrary animals. It was no easy task. Under normal circumstances, it was tough work. It was not for the fainthearted.

WATERING

Growing crops in Old Testament Israel was a challenge. The country's location between the Mediterranean Sea and the desert produced unpredictable rainfall. Large areas were dry and barren, with stony terrain and only occasional rain. Some places were impossible to farm.

The soil was rich throughout the country, but the absence or shortage of rain made it necessary for farmers to catch water in cisterns of stone. The "early rains" came in late October and early November. The "latter rain" came in March and April, just before harvest. During the interim, if rainfall was scarce, the farmers used a type of dipper on a long pole to lift water from the cistern and direct it into hand-dug ditches and rills that would take it to the crops. Keeping the growing plants watered was a backbreaking task.

The Israelite farmer well understood the truth of Genesis 3:19: "In the sweat of your face you shall eat bread."

WEEDING

When the farmer grew grain crops, he might allow weeds to grow along with the barley or wheat. In the New Testament parable of the wheat and tares, it was explained that a separation would take place at the time of harvest. But the Israelites of Amos's day also grew beans, cucumbers, garlic, leeks, onions, and lentils. Weeds could not be permitted to overtake these vegetable crops, robbing them of soil nourishment and water.

Vineyards, too, required seasonal weeding before the grapes were harvested. The beautiful Song of the Vineyard in Isaiah 5 tells of the care needed and the implements used to keep the vineyard clear.

The farmer, his wife, his children, and hired help were kept busy pulling weeds by hand or chopping them with a primitive hoe. The time between sowing and harvesting was occupied constantly with work—hard, demanding work.

WAITING

Under usual circumstances, the period between when the seeds are placed in the earth and the time the yield is produced is a time spent in working, watering, weeding, and waiting. Growth—by the laws of nature—requires sunshine, water, and the passing of time. "For the earth yields crops by itself: first the blade, then the head, after that the full grain in the head" (Mark 4:28).

This is the normal process, but there is nothing normal about the Amos 9:13 season.

Often we give ourselves to what I call the "Worry of Waiting." Most of us handle anything better than the anxiety that comes with waiting. For most, the second hand on the clock moves too slowly, and for others the battery has completely died. We find ourselves in a time warp of longing for unfulfilled dreams. Our questions to God can be wrapped up in one word. "When?"

"Lord, I can handle the working, watering, and weeding, but I have to ask you, "When?"

You dedicated your children to God when they were babies. Promises from God's Word have been your comfort through the years as you watched them struggle with temptation, sin, and wrong decisions. Frequently, you have found yourself asking "When?"

You know all the verses of Scripture that apply to your need for patience. You quote them often, but you're still left with the question, "When?"

You regularly rehearse the meaningful words found in Isaiah 40:31 that read: "They that wait upon the Lord shall renew their strength; they shall mount up with wings as eagles; they shall run and not be weary; and they shall walk and not faint" (KJV).

Still you ask, "When?"

You remember the words of Paul in Romans 8:18 about how life's current sufferings are minimal when compared to our future glory, but you still have to know, "When?"

You memorized the entire third chapter of Ecclesiastes and you are well aware of the fact that everything has a season, but in exasperation, you ask … "When?"

David asked a similar question in Psalm 119:84 when he inquired, "How long must your servant wait?"

Job's wife asked it in Job 2:9, "How long will you cling to your integrity. Curse God and die."

Joseph must have asked it a thousand times in the prison. "When?" "How long?"

You've asked it standing in the hospital hallway or maybe you pondered it leaving the cemetery graveside service. Why? When?

Everyone expects those grueling and stressful seasons of waiting.

This is the normal process, but there is nothing normal about the Amos 9:13 season. In the Amos 9:13 season . . .

- You will encounter greater favor.
- You will experience greater faith.
- You will engage a greater focus.
- You will embark on a greater future.
- You will enjoy greater fulfillment.

The Amos 9:13 season represents a new paradigm where supernatural living becomes the daily expectation. It is a paradigm of expanded boundaries of faith that allow for Kingdom expansion and accomplishment. It's a paradigm that will prepare God's kingdom children to transition into the coming millennial reign where every nation, government, and economy rest upon the shoulders of the righteous King.

The Amos 9:13 season is a time when "normal" will be redefined by Kingdom expectations.

The typical attitude of "the least you can expect" kind of life, just took a mega leap forward.

6

The Pace of Grace

An amazing story nestled in the pages of the sixth chapter of 2 Kings reveals what I call the miraculous "pace of grace" that comes with God's intervention. In the throes of a crippling famine, when conditions just couldn't get any worse, deliverance came with only a day's notice. With the deliverance came sudden wealth and provision that revived a nation and set the course for their prosperous future. The entire chapter speaks of accelerated provision and favor, and merits our study and consideration.

Second Kings 6 actually contains three stories. Each story, standing alone and separate, is a powerful account of God's power. However, when linked together, they crescendo into one of those Amos 9:13 types of "make your head swim" miracles.

THE SWIMMING AX HEAD

The chapter opens with the account of the young sons of the prophets who had determined their dwelling and learning facilities needed to be enlarged. One of them borrowed an ax and was busy chopping at a tree when the cutting blade became dislodged from the handle and fell into a small pond near the worksite. Being made of iron, of course, it sank to the bottom. Now, I have great admiration for the young man for what he did. However, I applaud him most for what he didn't do.

He did not merely continue to go through the motions. He understood that to keep striking the bark of the tree with the blunt end of a stick was nothing more than an exercise in futility. It was best to stop and deal with the problem by running to his spiritual authority, Elisha, and from him request helpful intervention. What powerful lessons and parallels are contained in this young preacher's response!

How have you reacted in the past upon discovering your cutting edge was missing; when the prayer closet was no longer compelling; and praise became a chore? What did you do, Pastor, when preaching became a duty and preparation became nothing but cumbersome? Too many just keep chopping away with the blunt end of a proverbial stick with no effectiveness whatsoever. Often, some have mistakenly thought that singing faster songs, jumping higher, and shouting louder would get the job done just the same, but I'm reminded of what Paul wrote to the Galatian Christians in Galatians 3:3: "Are ye so foolish? Having begun in the Spirit, are you now made perfect by the flesh?" (KJV).

The best solution for lost effectiveness is to quit wasting precious time and energy with fleshly exertions, and run and yield to a higher authority than you to plead for help.

When the young man found Elisha, he was confronted with a simple question, yet encased within the question was a profound truth. The probing question was "Where did it fall?" (2 Kings 6:6). The profound truth was this:

"You'll find it where you lost it." At some point, one has to be confronted with the question of spiritual inventory. What were you doing when you noticed something was missing in your life? Were your habits hindering your productivity? Was the company you were keeping or possibly the entertainment to which you were giving yourself displeasing the Lord? Have you learned how to preach past the conviction and maneuver your way around the spiritual alarm your heart was experiencing? Gone is the exhilarating thrill of it all, and the only thing you have left is the jarring frustration of hitting at your target with the blunt end of old sermons and songs.

Don't take my word alone. Just ask Samson. He still looked like a strong man. All the signs were still there. Only when he awakened from the compromising relationship with Delilah did he realize his strength had come from a higher and holier source than his lifestyle could accommodate. Samson and a host of others would tell you the only answer is to stop. Please stop. Don't waste any more time. Run to the Lord and cry for help.

Once Elisha and the apprentice prophet returned to the worksite, the older prophet tossed a stick into the water and the iron ax head surfaced. What a miracle to consider! This heavy iron blade suddenly became buoyant and floated near where the two prophets were standing. Reaching down into the water, they retrieved the ax head, reattached it to the handle, and finished the job of cutting down the tree.

Your loss of effective and powerful living need not be permanent. You still have a future. There's something that can be "thrown" into the depths of your circumstances that can give buoyancy to your anointing. When is the last time you pitched the cross into the depths of your problem? That old piece of wood has been bringing things to the surface for a long time. I have good news for you today—your gift is about to resurface, and when it does, you must get a new grip on it. Once again, attach it to your life and complete the work the Father has given you to do.

SEEING THROUGH EYES OF REVELATION

Without segue, the sixth chapter of 2 Kings leaps right into a most interesting account of Kingdom insight. Something similar to the spiritual gift known as the "word of knowledge" seems to be at work in this story. It appears that each time the King of Syria developed a strategy to battle against the people of God, his plans were made known before he could initiate them. At first, he suspected his counselors and other trusted members of his cabinet, and accused them of betrayal. However, when he learned Elisha with his prophetic gift was responsible, the king called for his arrest and imprisonment. He then dispatched a large regiment of soldiers to the city of Dothan to retrieve the prophet and his servant.

Can you see the enemy's use of intimidation here? Hundreds of soldiers postured against only two of the Lord's servants. It's an age-old tactic Satan has employed over and over again. Early one morning, Elisha's servant stepped outside and discovered they were surrounded by Syrian soldiers. Frozen by fear, he stared at the enemy for a moment, and then ran into the house to announce the dilemma to Elisha. The prophet refused to be gripped by the servant's panic. He simply prayed for God to open the eyes of the servant so he might have the full revelation that had been veiled behind fact and reality. You see, the fact of the matter emphatically announced, "You are surrounded." The revelation behind that fact was this, "Those who are with us are more than those who are with them" (2 Kings 6:16).

You've possibly known the facts affecting your life for a long time, but have you ever considered the revelation of God's plan and purpose behind them? On any given day, the various bearers of fact will come in and out of your life. Doctors, lawyers, counselors, or any other number of people can load you down with the facts, but how liberating it is when the revelation of grace and provision sweep in, bringing hope for tomorrow.

As God was opening the eyes of revelation for Elisha's servant, he blinded the eyes of the Syrian soldiers. In that instant, the enemy became subjected to God's overwhelming power. Always remember that the enemy of your harvest can never compete with the greater purpose that has already been established and provided in God's plan for you.

I fully believe the Amos 9:13 season holds incredible insight for those who will focus on the harvest. Through the Spirit, you will see and observe things you've never been aware of before. You will become acutely aware of harvest opportunities and, as a result, you will give laser-beam focus to harvest strategy and Kingdom advancement. The scales will fall from your eyes and no longer will you be diverted from fulfilling the destiny into which you were called. You are about to come into a prophetic perception that will confound evil forces.

7

A Day of
Divine Intervention

In a word, the Amos 9:13 season is about "intervention." Make that, "divine intervention." Who but
God could so dramatically affect nature that an entire season adjusts to His purpose and design? After all, He made the seas to part and stand at attention
as a nation marched through to their deliverance. God
placed time on "pause" without disrupting the earth's
orbit, so much so that Joshua had to acknowledge the
sun stood still long enough for him to fight and win a
battle against his enemies. He adjusted time for an ailing
king by putting the day in reverse; only the position of
the sundial could adequately testify to the phenomenal
interruption of the norm, while Hezekiah made plans
for the additional 15 years granted to him by God.

Our Lord is the infinite God who cannot be held
captive by the clock or calendar. Time with all its sup-
pressing limits is ultimately at the mercy of the only and
eternal God who will never be threatened nor bullied

by the impossibilities of your life's circumstances. The latter half of the story contained in 2 Kings 6 reveals this wonderful truth.

As the servant of Elisha was experiencing the eye-opening revelation, the Syrian army was stricken with blindness. Groping in darkness, they were led by Elisha to Samaria and given over to the king. Rather than inflicting revenge upon their enemies, Elisha instructed the king that they be given food and released to return to Syria where they would be reunited with family. One of the greatest biblical examples of grace is seen in these actions of benevolence toward the enemies of Samaria. I tend to think that following such a display of kindness, the Syrian king would never have threatened Samaria again, but a seemingly insignificant phrase links all of the preceding stories of 2 Kings 6 to the last one. It's the phrase, "After this."

AFTER THIS

"And it came to pass after this, that King Benhadad, king of Syria, gathered all his host, and went up, and besieged Samaria" (2 Kings 6:24 KJV).

Think about that for a moment.

Great kindness had been shown ... but, "after this."

A large regiment of soldiers healed of sudden blindness and set free to return home ... but, "after this."

One would think after such a display of mercy, the Syrians would have been content to at least have peaceful coexistence with the people of Samaria. But that notion is destroyed with the introduction of all that comes with the phrase, "After this."

How many "after-this" occasions have you had when on the heels of great victories you encountered the vicious attack of satanic forces?

I must state here that the Amos 9:13 season is not without its detractors, enemies, and hindrances. Years ago, I heard one of my long-distance preaching mentors, Adrian Rogers, say, "When God starts blessing, Satan starts blasting." Count on it. But count on this as well—"When the enemy comes in like a flood, the Spirit of the Lord will lift up a standard against him" (Isaiah 59:19).

SURROUNDED BY THE SON
OF THE THUNDERER

King Benhadad was a wicked bully. He was a conniving tyrant. He was a sadistic monarch. His name means "The Son of the Thunderer." That just sounds mean. Even after all the mercy extended to his army, he commanded them to go and besiege the city of Samaria. It's important to understand there was a vital difference between attacking and besieging a city. Attacking a city denoted the inflicting of pain, resulting in bloodshed. It typically meant barging through the gates and taking no prisoners. However, when a city was besieged, it was surrounded on every side. The plan of Benhadad was to separate the city from its harvest by employing a strategy of containment. As a result, the export and import of the city was stopped, the harvest fields couldn't be reached, and soon a "man-made" famine existed. The famine described later in this story was not the result of drought or a failed harvest. Rain had come recently, and the fields were full of grain; but Samaria couldn't get to it because of a stubborn enemy.

This is yet another age-old strategy of Satan against the church. He takes great delight in besieging the church, containing it, and ultimately separating it from its harvest. Any famine the church experiences will never be due to a lack of rain or a failed harvest. It's been raining since the Day of Pentecost when the prophecy of Joel 2:28 was fulfilled.

God said in this passage, "I will pour out my Spirit upon all flesh; and your sons and your daughters shall prophesy" (Joel 2:28 KJV). In Hosea's writings, the promise of rain was foretold again. "And he shall come to us as the rain, as the latter and former rain unto the earth" (Hosea 6:3).

Famine in the church will never be the fault of an insufficient harvest either. There is an abundant harvest to be reaped in every direction. In Matthew 9:37, Jesus clearly stated to the disciples that the harvest was "plenteous." The culprit of any famine in this day of abundant rain and available harvest can only be the scheme of the Enemy perpetuated in strategic phases of implementation.

The church has been besieged by compromise, surrounded by selfish attitudes, and contained by lukewarmness. As a result, the church has taken on a containment mentality and a survivalist posture fed by desperation.

THE SURVIVALIST POSTURE

In the throes of the economic meltdown of 2008, former mayor of Jacksonville, Florida, John Payton, made the following statement: "We cannot let the existing climate create a survivalist thinking or paralysis."

The desperation fostered by a survivalist posture that came to Samaria led its citizens' appetite to three horrific food staples. The accounts given in 2 Kings 6 convey a story of times so terrible and people so hungry that they were consuming the heads of donkeys, dove dung, and most tragically of all, their own children.

The nutritional value in a donkey's head is as limited as the meat it supplies. However, their consumption of such a thing says more of the stubborn and relentless circumstances that forced the people to such tasteless, and possibly even biblically-forbidden, action (Leviticus

64

11:3-4). Much like the resistant and stubborn nature of a donkey, the famine that had come to Samaria had set in for a while.

Those who couldn't afford to purchase a donkey's head for 80 shekels of silver (that's $2,080 in 2014 value) were left to eat the dung of the dove. How humiliating this must have been for anyone of human pride and etiquette to consider doing. How difficult to even think of such a thing, but consider the following application of their actions.

The waste of the dove was symbolic of its past experience. It represented where the dove had been, what it had eaten, and now eliminated from its body. In other words, the people of Samaria were feasting on the "past." How amazing to consider. A church or a people enduring a spiritual famine can dine only on where it has been in its past, because it has no relevant present or compelling future. They attempt to recapture a meaningful memory with an old hymn from yesteryear. Often a famine-stricken church will continue to operate from old paradigms of ancient days, hoping those same methods will produce at least similar results, only to be disappointed time and again. However, to those who will accept it, God is doing a new thing and its sustaining nutrition is energizing and strengthening all who believe.

Samaria was more than hungry. They were famished to the point of desperation.

THE DANGER OF DESPERATION

The word *desperation* is defined as "the loss of hope and surrender to despair." Desperate people do desperate things that have no foundation in anything that resembles logic. I don't know that desperation is played out any more graphically anywhere else in the Bible than in the latter portion of 2 Kings 6.

65

As a desperate king walked and surveyed his traumatized city one day, he gave attention to the plea for help from a heartbroken mother. The story she told him would capture anybody. Let me take it directly from the scripture.

"The king said to her, 'What is troubling you?' "

"She answered, 'This woman said to me, give your son, that we may eat him today and we will eat my son tomorrow.' So we boiled my son, and ate him: and I said to her on the next day, 'Give your son, that we may eat him: but she has hidden her son'" (2 Kings 6:28-29).

There are tremendous spiritual implications throughout this unimaginable story. Caught somewhere between desperation and survivability, the church has too often eaten its seed in an immediate moment of crises, while unknowingly bankrupting itself of any of tomorrow's dreams and potential. Wherever spiritual famine exists, it must be broken or else our sons and daughters will pay the extreme price of being basted in the fires of our own carnal hunger and survivalist mentality.

Moved by the woman's story, the king tore his garments and revealed he was wearing sackcloth underneath his robes. Typically, this would have been seen as a sign of repentance and humility. However, in this case, the king's act is only an outward display lacking inward sincerity. His own words of contempt toward Elisha are proof of his heart's real condition. You can read it here.

"God do so to me and more also, if the head of Elisha the son of Shaphat remains on him today" (2 Kings 6:31).

One sure sign of needed intervention is when someone, especially in leadership, refuses to take responsibility for his condition. When an individual won't allow himself to see the seriousness of impending calamity, there is a need for intervention. The king couldn't get past his seething hatred and animosity against Elisha.

The sackcloth he was wearing had no effect on his need for the true repentance he should have embraced.

The famine drags on as the sixth chapter comes to a close. The last picture given in this chapter is Elisha and the elders of the city sitting with him in his house, when the city is in a chaotic fit. That little "Oh, by the way" description of his reclining position shouldn't be overlooked. While others are frantic, Elisha and his elders are calm. While others are pacing, Elisha is patiently waiting. He anticipated the change of seasons was coming. Others had taken the posture of panic, but Elisha is in a relaxed position and from that position and posture, he takes command and becomes the voice of reason in what had been an unreasonable climate. In a moment of bold "This has gone on long enough" fervor, Elisha stands and declares: "By this time tomorrow, the famine will be over."

Oh, for another prophetically aligned moment like that where men and women of God are given the voice of authority and power that calms troubled hearts and eases perplexed minds. When Washington, D.C., is confused and Wall Street is in convulsions and the dark clouds of despair loom close to the earth, maintain your posture of peace. Intervention is coming. The season is changing.

The prophet Daniel said it best, "Blessed be the name of God forever and ever: for wisdom and might are His: He changes the times and the seasons: He removes kings, and raises up kings: He gives wisdom to the wise, and knowledge to those who have understanding" (Daniel 2:20-21).

The winds are shifting. The cold and winter-like temperatures of adversity are yielding to the soul-reviving breezes of favor and blessing. Be assured, God does change the seasons.

He always has.

He still does.

8

The Difference
a Day Makes

It doesn't take many words to announce the oncoming of a new season, if it's the right word from the start. Elisha postured himself somewhere between despair and anguish, and with the use of one primary word, became an ambassador of deliverance, declaring prosperity was only a day away. He intentionally selected the word "tomorrow" to ignite hope in the hearts of those who heard him. Imagine the emotional flood that washed over the hungry and heartbroken people of Samaria when God's prophet uttered his message.

"Listen! God's word! The famine's over. This time tomorrow food will be plentiful—a handful of meal for a shekel; two handfuls of grain for a shekel. The market at the city gate will be buzzing" (2 Kings 7:1 MSG).

With one word, a kingdom was transformed from their dilemma into their deliverance. Within 24 hours they had a new currency, a new diet, but more than anything else, they had new hope. Only God could have orchestrated the series of events that led to their dramatic resurrection from the throes of death itself.

The day began with no noticeable difference than the day before. The citizens of Samaria were as hungry at sunrise as they had been at sundown the evening earlier. Meanwhile, outside the gates of the city where the lepers and other outcasts had been exiled, a dreadful realization had dawned with the morning. No food would be provided any longer for those considered to be in worse condition than those within the walled city of Samaria.

Among the hopeless were four lepers engaged in a most insightful conversation. They concluded there were no good options that would bring relief to their situation. To call upon family and friends within the city for food meant certain starvation. The other choice was to give themselves to the Syrian army who had caused this problem in the first place. The lepers were wise enough to know they would be put to death by the Syrian soldiers, but they were hopeful enough to believe they would be allowed to eat before being killed. They rationalized that even though they would likely be put to death, at least they wouldn't die hungry. Sometimes the choices just aren't very good, and like the four lepers, you analyze the options only to realize none of them are really viable.

WHY SIT WE HERE?

Of all their considerations, the lepers knew one thing for certain. What they had been doing wasn't working anymore and something had to change. Their conclusion inspires and motivates me. You see, in order to inaugurate the oncoming of a new season, at some point, the old season has to be left behind. The lepers said to one another, "Why sit we here until we die?" (2 Kings 7:3 KJV). I can almost hear one of them say to the others,

"Whatever this is, it just isn't working anymore." We all have to face that truth before we can enter in to a new season. I learned long ago that before I can move into my future, my future has to move into me. Many times a new season is precipitated by our own actions of faith.

There's a good reason why Jesus would often require an initial act of faith on the part of someone in need of a miracle. You hear it in His commands.

To the man with a withered hand, Jesus said "Stretch forth thine hand" (Matthew 12:13 KJV).

To the man at the Pool of Bethesda, He said "Take up your bed, and walk" (John 5:8).

To the blind man, the Master said "Go wash in the pool of Siloam" ((John 9:7).

Peter walked to Jesus on the water only after he obeyed the Lord's command to step out of the boat (Matthew 14:29).

The message behind every command to stretch forth, rise up, or step out was simply this, "You will never change what you are willing to tolerate." Understand this: God will not impose the Amos 9:13 season on anyone. To tolerate misery is to miss opportunity. To put up with mediocrity is to miss destiny. At some point, logistical inventory has to be considered and the question, "Why am I still sitting here?" has to be asked and answered.

THE SOUND OF FAITH

Four leprous men finally stood and balanced themselves upon their leprous limbs and began to do the only thing they knew—walk.

That was it; they just walked.

They walked in faith and hope. They moved with determination and expectancy. Motivated by the aroma of

71

the bread, these four men soon found themselves marching as if to the steady cadence of a loud drum. However, in reality, their footsteps were hardly making any noise at all as they moved across the field toward the Syrian army. That was only in the natural and visible realm. But in the invisible and spiritual realm, their footsteps were shaking the kingdom of darkness. According to God's Word in 2 Kings 7:6, the four leprous men produced a sound similar to an approaching army.

> "For the Lord had made the host of the Syrians to hear a noise of chariots, and a noise of horses, even the noise of a great host: and they said one to another, 'Look, the king of Israel hath hired against us the kings of the Hittites, and the kings of the Egyptians, to come upon us" (KJV).

By their own admission, the Syrians acknowledged that the steps of the eight feet of four lepers sounded like three invading armies coming against them. Upon hearing the sound of what seemed to be an overwhelming army, the enemy ran away, leaving behind the gold and silver. Most important, they left behind the bread and seed for another harvest.

Our Heavenly Father always adds volume to our acts of obedience. In this natural world, much of what we do in faith isn't noticed at all, but be assured that invisible kingdoms are being impacted. There's a sound to your gifts when they fall in the offering plates on Sunday mornings at church. There's a sound louder than you realize in your faint midnight-hour petition to God. There's a thunderous roar to your praise that pushes back against Satan's forces. That's why Joshua commanded the children of Israel to shout and blow trumpets at Jericho. That's why Gideon commanded 300 men to shout and blow trumpets when attacking the Midianites. That's why David wrote in Psalm 47:1, "Oh clap your hands, all ye people; shout unto God with a voice of triumph" (KJV). It's the sound of faith!

GO TELL THE CITY

As the lepers entered the Syrian camp, they discovered the enemy had fled, but had left behind everything necessary to break a famine. Imagine the scene.

Four sick beggars with what seemed to be a death wish, walked into a large camp and found it vacant. Nothing left except enough food and treasure to resurrect the all but dead city of Samaria. They began to devour the food and throw gold coins in the air, watching them fall back to the ground like rain drops. Several minutes of euphoric splendor passed when one of them stopped his celebrating. Looking at the others, he said, "This isn't right that we enjoy all this bounty while our brothers and sisters are starving in Samaria. Let's return and share the good news."

It must have been like the old miners in the gold rush days trying to walk into town to stake their claim. The smile on their faces told all there was to tell. As soon as the lepers neared the gates of Samaria and the hungry people saw them using their sleeves to wipe away the breadcrumbs from their mouths, the rush was on. A human stampede ran through the gates, out to the field, and into the enemy's vacant camp. In that instant, the season changed and the famine was over.

There is someone whose season will not change until they hear the good news, and having obtained such great victory, my responsibility as well as yours is to now become a catalyst of change in someone's life. One of the greatest descriptions of evangelism I ever heard was from Missiologist D.T. Niles: "Sharing the Good News is simply one beggar telling another beggar where he found bread."

Paul wrote in 2 Corinthians 5:18-20a:

> Now all things are of God, who hath reconciled us
> to Himself through Jesus Christ, and has given us
> the ministry of reconciliation, that is, that God was
> in Christ reconciling the world to Himself, not im-
> puting their trespasses to them, and has committed
> to us the word of reconciliation. Now we are am-
> bassadors for Christ, as though God were pleading
> through us.

God chooses to use you to speak on His behalf and tell
the world the famine is over and the reasons for rejoic-
ing can be found everywhere.

9

The Hellacious Middle

I'm not sure who said it first, but it's true and I've lived it out a time or two myself. "When God shuts a door, He opens another, but sometimes it's hell in the hallway." There are probably more dignified ways to say it, but if you've ever experienced it for yourself, then you know there's really no better way to describe it. It's what I call the "Hellacious Middle," the transitional place of the "in-between"—that season between your birth and your destiny.

We see it throughout the Bible.

Joseph experienced it in the pit and the prison before reaching the palace. Then there is Job. His story is told in 42 chapters in the Bible, but 37 of them are used to describe his troubles and the ensuing charges and accusations of his friends. Finally, in Chapter 38, God starts talking and things change dramatically. Similar stories could be told about Abraham, Moses, Paul, and many others.

A story from an experience in David's life best illustrates the difficulties we can encounter on the road to our "season of favor." David was born in Bethlehem and ultimately ruled during a fruitful season as king from Jerusalem for most of 40 years; but prior to his coronation, he had the Ziklag experience. Ziklag was a town located in the Negev region in the south of what was the kingdom of Judah.

In the biblical account of 1 Samuel 30, David and his men returned to Ziklag from being temporarily aligned with the Philistine army. Coming into the city, David and his men immediately discovered the Amalekites had demolished the city, set it afire, and captured all the people, including David's family. Talk about the worst day of a man's life—this may have been it for David. He lost his family, his home, and suffered bankruptcy all in one day. Now that's a bad day.

Look at the effects it had on David and his men.

> Then David and the people who were with him lifted up their voices and wept until they had no more power to weep . . . David was greatly distressed; for the people spoke of stoning him, because the soul of all the people was grieved, every man for his sons and for his daughters (1 Samuel 30:4, 6).

It had to be next to impossible to imagine a throne in Jerusalem while standing in the ash heaps of Ziklag. That "Hellacious Middle" seems like more than just a phase when you're going through it. It often seems like the final stop and the last destination when your tears won't subside and your problems won't end. Indeed, this ranks as being one of the worst, if not the very worst day of David's life.

Have you ever been there? What do you do on what seems to be the worst day of your life—when that season of seemingly unending trouble hangs over you like a fog that never dissipates?

Using David as an example, allow me to lift some lessons from his response to his Ziklag experience. What did he do, and what should you do on what may be the worst day of your life?

DAVID WEPT

It's hard to avoid it. Weeping comes naturally and should be allowed for you and others close to you. Jesus did it at the tomb of Lazarus. Abraham cried upon Sarah's passing. Peter wept bitterly when the impact of his betraying Jesus fully hit him. Weeping is a natural and human response. It has its place with everyone, even Christians. The walk of faith is not a walk without feelings. Maybe life would be simpler if we had to deal with only "the facts," but we also must learn to cope with the "feelings of our infirmities" as well. There is an emotion that comes with being sick, and there are feelings that come with being disappointed. It's all part of the healing process.

According to the Bible, in Ecclesiastes 3:4, "There is a time to mourn." It has its place, because God created us as emotional beings. Weeping is not inconsistent with faith, but after weeping for a season, there comes a time to take some steps toward strength and well-being.

Once when visiting a hospital, I talked with a man who had just experienced corrective surgery. He informed me that while the surgery was painful in and of itself, the greater pain came when the physical therapist came to his room to help him walk for the first time following the procedure. The pain to that new knee brought on by those first few steps was almost unbearable. However, the therapist knew that exercise was necessary in order to keep the infection at bay. The bending became a blessing, and the stretching became a source of strength. I walked away from that conversation understanding that sometimes it hurts to heal.

Admittedly, there are many things in life that to simply relegate them to a "just get over it" attitude will never suffice, but we do have to learn to be able to take those first steps down the hallway again. You may grimace and groan, and a tear may escape the corner of your eyes occasionally, but you will recover your stride again. David did. Others have, and so will you. Like the lepers referred to in another chapter, you have to ask yourself the question, "Why will I sit here until I die?" Get up and move toward your next season.

DAVID WORSHIPED

Sorry to ruin your fun and end any pity party you may have reserved, but the weeping has to end and the worship must begin. If it doesn't, you will further delay your arrival into your favored season and destiny. Taking a close look at David's response to the trial at Ziklag, you will discover that while others were giving in to immediate bitterness, he resisted that temptation and focused on the Lord. There is a real treasure of meaning in this verse. Look at it carefully:

> "David was greatly distressed; for the people spoke of stoning him, because the soul of the people was grieved, every man for his sons and for his daughters: but David encouraged himself in the Lord his God" (1 Samuel 30:6, KJV).

The temptation to embrace bitterness and harbor grudges will be the first things to greet you when you're coming into your own burning Ziklag experience. It's another one of those emotively prompted responses we typically experience; however, it is one that must be curtailed and dealt with as early as possible in any trying experience. For David, it must have been a difficult thing to press through. He wasn't at fault, but he was being blamed by his army of distressed and depressed men. Bitterness and blame usually walk hand-in-hand, and David knew it, but he didn't recycle vengeance. He chose rather to lift it all up to God, trust Him with the outcome, wait, and worship. David saw the entire matter for what it really was, and so should you. The Ziklag incident was designed by the Enemy to keep David from getting to Jerusalem and reigning as king, and whatever is falling apart in your life right now is simply a roadblock to your destined season. Satan knows that if he can shut you up, he can shut you down—so worship. The choice has always been . . .

Pout or praise.

Moan or magnify.

Sigh or sing.

Bellyache in cynicism or break forth with singing.

David had it right. He encouraged himself in the Lord. How?

Being the songwriter that he was, possibly he recalled some of his songs and began to sing them unto the Lord. Maybe he reached for the old songbook of the soul and began to turn the pages.

I can almost hear him sing portions of Psalm 34: "I will bless the Lord at all times; His praise shall continually be in my mouth. My soul shall make its boast in the Lord; the humble shall hear of it and be glad. Oh, magnify the Lord with me, and let us exalt His name together" (Psalm 34:1 3).

Then he may have reflected on Psalm 27 and sang,

The Lord is my light and my salvation; whom shall I fear? The Lord is the strength of my life; of whom shall I be afraid? When the wicked came against me to eat up my flesh, my enemies and foes, they stumbled and fell. Though an army should encamp against me, my heart shall not fear; though

war should rise against me, in this I will be confi-
dent. . . . For in the time of trouble He shall hide me
in His pavilion; in the secret place of His tabernacle
He shall hide me; He shall set me high upon a rock
(Psalm 27:1 3, 5).

I think that's how he did it. Because when you're all
alone without any support system to sustain you, there
has to be an inner reservoir within your own spirit that
you can draw from. David had no one. His own men
were ready to kill him, but somehow he was able to focus on the good things of God and worship his way toward his new season.

Whatever you focus on will magnify. If you place the
magnifying glass of concentration over your problems,
your problems will become larger; but when that magnifying glass of concentration is placed upon the Lord,
then His power and glory become greater in your life.
Understand that looking at God through your magnifying glass of faith doesn't make Him bigger, because He
can't be improved upon, but it changes your perspective. Suddenly you see God as you've never seen Him
before. That's what worship does.

Over and over, throughout his life, David reaped the
benefits brought to him by his worshiping heart.

Paul understood the same principle of praising his
way into the next season. He had been beaten with rods,
snakebitten, shipwrecked, betrayed, and thrown into
prison, but in the midnight hour, he joined with Silas
and they sang their praises to God. God responded, the
earth quaked, the prison was opened, and a new season
was inaugurated in Paul's life.

I remember walking into my office early one Mon-
day morning with what seemed to be the weight of the
world on my shoulders. Our church was in the middle
of constructing a new building, and I had haggled over

contracts, met with committees and city inspectors to the point where I felt like a building contractor more than a preacher. I had schedules to keep, places to travel, and parishioners needing my attention. My own family needed me more than anyone or anything else. I had been there only a few minutes, slowly shuffling to my desk, when exhaustion overwhelmed me. The day before I had preached on praise and worship and had even made a point or two about dancing before the Lord as David did. The crowd responded, and we worshiped together in an exuberant manner. However, within 24 hours, I was depleted and empty. I knew that my ministry, as well as the church, was moving toward a new season of victory, but that morning it seemed far away. As I reflected on the worship experience that happened the day before, I sensed an impression of the Holy Spirit. I believed He was saying to me, "Can you do alone in this office what you did on the stage yesterday in front of all of those people?"

I must admit that it was a difficult thing to consider. There was no music and no crowd to worship with me. Besides, I didn't feel like *walking* across the floor, much less *singing* and *dancing* before the Lord. People were busy in the hallways, while others were waiting in the reception area to see me. A few cups of coffee and I'd be past it anyway, or so I reasoned, but the thought wouldn't leave me.

Could I worship him alone even in the dance?

"WOULD I DO IT ALONE?"

A dozen reasons for not dancing rushed in on me, but I slowly raised my hands in praise while sitting at my desk. Then I began to quote every verse of scripture I could recall. Soon the tears began to flow, and before I could talk myself out of it, I pushed back from the desk, stood up, and began to leap and dance. I learned later that my staff had gathered outside my door, listening to their pastor have what they surely must have thought was a breakdown; but when I walked out, they discovered that I had actually experienced a breakthrough in my spirit. Like David, I had learned how to encourage myself in the Lord.

What about you? Are you in the hallway between a closed and an open door? If you are, then this is the time to worship your Heavenly Father and encourage yourself in His Word, His favor, and His promise.

10

A Word in Season

One of the great life lessons I've learned is this: Never make permanent decisions based entirely on temporary circumstances. A close look at David's decisions during his Ziklag experience indicates that he, too, had learned the same thing.

A burning heap of rubble was all that remained of Ziklag as David and his men approached the city limits. With their wives and children taken away, nothing was left but a smoldering memory of what once had been. Such a circumstance would seem permanent to any observer, but while righteous indignation must have sprung up in David's heart, he found no place for a panicked response. This was not the time for careless and thoughtless reactions. His men were ready to go on a rampage of revengeful destruction, but David took measured steps of analyzed strategy before making his first move. While everyone was pulling at him for immediate vengeance to be inflicted upon their enemies, David put a hold on everything and said, "I need to hear from the Lord."

Scripture records in 1 Samuel 30:7 8 that David called

upon the priest and said, "Bring me the ephod." The ephod was a priestly garment used at times to seek the will of God. When it was brought it to him, David inquired of the Lord saying, 'Shall I pursue these raiders? Shall I overtake them?" And God answered him, 'Pursue, for you shall surely overtake them and without fail recover all" (v. 8).

A WORD FROM THE LORD

When it was needed most, David received a finely focused and personal word of direction from the Lord. This specific direction came as God's *rhema* word straight to David's heart for his situation. David employed the Old Testament means of utilizing the priest's ephod—a sacred garment associated with worship and typically worn by the high priest. It wouldn't be the only time David sent for it. He also called for it on the occasion of bringing the ark of the covenant back to Jerusalem.

Today, in this era of New Testament grace, the inspired Word of God and the abiding presence of the Holy Spirit in a Christian's heart makes the use of this garment unnecessary and obsolete. However, in Old Testament times, God himself had instructed Moses and Aaron in its original use, along with the multijeweled breastplate, and utilized them to help signal clear direction to His people. David realized that he had to receive a word from God, and it demanded total focus, great intentionality, along with self-imposed isolation to get it. Thus, he called for the ephod.

While old covenant attire with its numerous priestly accessories is now a thing of the past which is no longer required, you will discover that focus, self-denial, and solitude with God are still prerequisites if you ever wish to hear from Him. At some point, it becomes necessary for you to walk away from the noise of your surroundings, grasp hold of your Bible, shut the door behind you, and say, "God, it's just you and me and I can't to go any farther until you talk to my spirit from Your Word." Our Heavenly Father has made this promise to those who pursue Him: "You will seek me and find me, when you seek me with all your heart" (Jeremiah 29:13 NIV).

There are no shortcuts to this process. Occasionally, I meet someone who wants their "word" and they want it "now." They chase "words" on a frequent basis, attempting to get their "fix" in order to make it through one more day. Rather than consecrate themselves to prayer and the study of the Scriptures, they would rather accept what often could be no more than a random prognostication of a third party.

I well remember visiting a revival meeting several years ago. I had heard about the speaker and his well-advertised "flow" in spiritual gifts, and I wanted to learn more about his ministry. I was somewhat surprised when this minister called for me to come forward and receive the prophetic "word" he claimed to have for me. With much reluctance, I obediently moved forward and found myself standing before him. At that point, things got very interesting as he said to me, "Your sickness is not unto death." He had my attention. Now, I must admit that although I had been somewhat discouraged over a few matters I had been facing, physically, I was doing well and had a recent doctor's report to confirm it. I certainly had no clue that I had become terminal with some "unknown" malady. Immediately, I had an overwhelming desire to get out of the building before I was given another "word," but it was too late. He had another "word" installment for me. The auditorium was reverently quiet as everyone there listened to what the minister was speaking to me. Then he said it, "The Lord would have me say unto you, thou shalt not die as long as you live." With that, the people went wild with an ovation of thunderous applause, and I went home. I had learned about the minister all I really needed to know. Distributed throughout the body of Christ are scripturally authentic gifts, including the word of knowledge and word of wisdom. However, occasionally there will arise unqualified "wordsmiths" that may mean well, but have no scripturally legitimate foundation to stand upon when attempting to speak for God.

Know this: if and when God chooses to use someone to share a word specifically targeted to you and your need, it should flow from the firm and valid foundation of Scripture. Otherwise, it may be only conjecture and inventive thinking.

When David inquired of the Lord and received immediate instruction from Him, he understood the direction he received was flowing out of the Father's eternal Word, will, and Kingdom plan to secure victory for those called by His name.

A NEW VISION

The Lord's word to David came in response to his original two questions: "Shall I go?" and "Will I win?" God wasted no time or words with His response. His answer to David was, "Pursue and recover all." With that direction, David began to cast a new vision filled with hope and restoration.

Suddenly, all of David's men came out of their depressed and desperate state of mind and renewed their allegiance to their leader. Knowingly or unknowingly, they seized a principle of faith that proved to be the key that unlocked the door to their season. The principle is this: You must "see" with eyes of faith what you heard God "say" with ears of understanding. They began to "call those things that [were] not as though they were" (Romans 4:17 KJV).

When you begin to drape vision around what God says, then you are moving closer into your new season of victorious living.

In his mind, David could see his family restored before he ever found them. His soldiers saw their children safe again. They lifted their eyes from the scorched remains of yesterday and gazed upon the brilliant promise of ten thousand tomorrows. Leaping upon their horses, they rode toward a battle that was won before they shot the first arrow.

The scriptural account of the battle is thrilling:

> Then David attacked them from twilight until the evening of the next day. Not a man of them escaped, except four hundred young men who rode on camels and fled. So David recovered all that the Amalekites had carried away, and David rescued his two wives. And nothing of theirs was lacking, either small or great, sons or daughters, spoil or anything which they had taken from them. David recovered all (1 Samuel 30:17 19).

Looking back over this amazing story, I have come to realize that David's Ziklag season was more about where he was going than where he was at the time. Within three days of this battle, David became the recognized King over Judah and soon over all Israel. Satan's attack on you is a diversion. It's his attempt to rob you of your destined place in God.

SEE IT FOR WHAT IT IS

Looking back over my life, I have experienced what I identify as some primary seasons of tremendous Kingdom enablement. The secular world would identify them as promotions, but I see them for what they truly are. I have been blessed at some strategic times in my life to have been providentially aligned to participate in increased Kingdom expansion. I cite this to simply acknowledge that prior to every advancement there has been at least a brief interval of immense spiritual—and at times even human—confrontation, when my faith was extremely tried. In the past, I have waged war with the Enemy over various matters where compromise and negotiation were out of the question. Regardless of what I may have faced before, nothing arrests my soul like an attack on my family.

Paula and I are parents of three beautiful daughters now grown and enjoying their families and varied careers. Each of our girls is a story of God's wonderful and unique blessings in our lives, and they've each brought us tremendous joy through the years.

Like every family, we've had our dramas, too. Our family portraits, complete with smiling faces and formal poses, don't tell the whole story. That little Christmas postcard we sent out in 1993, showing us standing by a snowman with Paula holding our little Cocker Spaniel puppy and me sipping a steaming cup of hot chocolate, doesn't come close to describing everyday life. What I'm about to relay is a little more in line with the reality that most people experience.

We had just returned from the university commencement exercises on Saturday. One of our girls had graduated with a business degree, complete with a 4.0 grade point average over four years. She had even been selected to give one of the speeches about her university experience during the program. We laughed, had a cookout, and beamed with joy while handing over to her the keys to a new car. She had worked hard, and I was thankful we could give it to her.

On Sunday morning, she awakened early, packed the new car, and moved to Ohio where she quickly found a good job with a bank in Columbus. Gifted in music and an incredible lyricist, she began to write songs that caught the attention of a producer and promoter of rock music. It wasn't long before the call came that my daughter with the business degree and making good money would now be joining and traveling with a rock band. Success came quickly as they acquired recording contracts complete with tours throughout the United States, Canada, and Europe. Though extremely proud of her talent and elated at her ability to write, our hearts became heavy as we followed her tour schedule on the Internet, realizing the kinds of venues where she was performing. Often were the nights that Paula sensed alarm in her spirit and would find her way to our child's bedroom and fall across the bed with tearful intercession. She did it so frequently that on the occasions when our daughter would visit us at home, she would ask about the smell of Paula's perfume emanating from the bed.

According to the press releases and CD reviews, they were attracting a good fan base; meanwhile, for four years while Paula and I traveled around the world preaching and giving altar calls so other people's children could be saved, in our minds and hearts, we were fighting a war for the soul of our own daughter.

More than once while I was preaching or carrying out church business, I was under a barrage of heat-seeking missiles of condemnation from the Enemy. I remember one night in Spain watching as hundreds of young people responded to the opportunity I extended for them to come to know Christ. While I rejoiced at that moment, I later went to my hotel room and muffled my groanings in a pillow as I wept for my child. I could only find sleep after reading aloud every scripture I could find about household salvation, and then claiming them as personal promises for my own family.

Four years went by. Four years of Paula walking down the hall and falling across that bed. Four years of my following the band's tour on their website and then wishing I hadn't, because I'd rather not have known the kind of places they were playing. Four years of putting on the face and taking a deep breath before walking on a stage to try to help somebody get through their spiritual Ziklag.

SOME THINGS ARE ABOUT YOUR ENDURANCE

Another lesson I've learned along the way is this: There are some things you'll go through that are more about your endurance than your achievement. Like David, we often inquired of the Lord. In those moments, Paula and I found the drive to keep praying and carrying on our ministry to others.

Then something happened just days after my early morning encounter when I received the Amos 9:13 promise of expedient favor and accelerated blessings. To this day, I don't know exactly what it was. I don't have to know and haven't ever asked. What I do know is that one day, my daughter called home and relayed to her mother that the band was ending.

She then began to unfold a dramatic encounter with Jesus that came as a result of a friend's testimony of grace in her own life. It wasn't long until our daughter returned home and began a journey of discipleship that has renewed her faith, as well as our own joy in the Lord.

Whatever your struggle may be today, see it for what it is. It's a hellacious middle between where you've been and where you're destined to be. Your season is about to change, and the Enemy and struggles you have today only verifies it. Four little words describe the tremendous victory that David experienced over the Amalekites. Four small words that ring with triumph: "And David recovered all."

The Amos 9:13 season is about recovery and God-ordained reversal. What the evil one designed for your harm and ultimate destruction will be repealed by the intervening power of your Heavenly Father. You, too, shall recover all!

11

Paradigm Paralysis

I've often said, "Before you can move into your future, your future must move into you." Meaning, the desire you have for a brighter tomorrow must so motivate you today that your vision for a better life becomes activated by your willingness to adjust. Be assured, time waits for no one and steadily marches to the unending cadence of change.

The inability of some people to see beyond current models of thinking and methods of "doing" have left them with paradigm paralysis. They are stuck in patterns and systems of operation that have, at best, rendered them deficient and at worst, dysfunctional.

Recently, I was thinking about some things made obsolete because of the advance in technology. I was amazed and amused at the same time. Amazed at what seems to be their near extinction and amused at the reliance I once had on them. Here are a few that came to mind:

- Public pay phones
- Cassette tapes

- VCRs and VHS cassettes
- Road maps
- Operator-assisted phone calls
- Printed encyclopedias
- Printed dictionaries
- Pagers
- Electric typewriters
- Camera film
- The need to instruct a service station attendant to "fill 'er up!"
- The need to collect the tickets from a travel agent's office.

This list, and its accompanying memories, brought a smile to my face as I wrote it down.

A LIST OF LOSS

Sadly, there are lists of a more serious nature that many people are making today. The list is created by those whose hearts are broken, their lives interrupted, and put on hold; it is a "list of loss" so great that it beggars description. Life as they knew it doesn't exist any longer. People whom they loved are gone, and relationships once cherished have vanished. For them, there are too many things they no longer have or do, but their desire for them never goes away.

Given enough time, grace, and a legitimate coping strategy, a person is usually able to carry on with life, but the crippling effects of loss are not easy to recover from. Rose Kennedy is attributed with the statement: "It has been said, 'Time heals all wounds.' I do not agree. The wounds remain. In time, the mind, protecting its sanity, covers them with scar tissue and the pain lessens, but it is never gone."

Whatever the case, loss will force at least a few alterations. To sit through change without at least some adaptation is to ignore the reality of your circumstances and miss the opportunity for meaningful transformation.

I have always found inspiration in the Bible story of Ruth and Naomi, and have told it over and over through the years. Actually, Ruth is one of my favorite books in the Bible. My heart is moved when I read about the loss Naomi suffered after leaving her hometown of Bethlehem with her husband and two sons. She probably didn't want to leave, but submitted to her husband Elimelech's wishes to put the woes of a famine-stricken land behind them. Interestingly, the name *Bethlehem* means "house of bread," but the meaning of a name and the reality of the circumstances were worlds apart. A paradigm of hunger and hopelessness marked the city, and Naomi's husband said, "I'm leaving, and you and the boys are coming with me." For 10 years, they journeyed through Moab, and during that span of time, Elimelech died, leaving Naomi to care for their two sons alone. Within a decade, the sons also died, shortly after marrying two young girls from Moab. By her own admission, Naomi was growing bitter from her losses, and to add insult to injury, her daughter-in-law, Orpah, seemed to forsake her at a difficult time.

Ten years earlier, Naomi and her family attempted to flee the paradigm of famine only to enter another one; the paradigm of deprivation and bereavement. Following the funeral of her last son, Naomi received news that the famine in Bethlehem had ended, and she purposed to return as soon as she possibly could. Naomi wouldn't have to travel alone, because Ruth vowed she would never leave Naomi and would embrace her people, as well as her God.

After a long journey, Naomi and Ruth entered Bethlehem and were met with the comments and stares of family and friends who had not seen Naomi in 10 years. They must have wondered about the beautiful young woman who had accompanied her and what role Ruth had played in Naomi's family. More than anything, they pondered what 10 years had done to Naomi.

Talking among themselves, Naomi's friends might have said: "Look, Naomi is back in town," and "Hasn't time taken its toll on her?"

Others possibly commented about the harshness of the years on Naomi's complexion and posture. It could have been Naomi's walk was slow and her shoulders were stooped from the long journey home. Gone was the smile of Naomi's youth, along with the good-natured demeanor of her personality. Why, even during the famine, they remembered how pleasant she was. After all, that's what her name meant; "good and pleasant" — but not now.

STUCK IN A PREVIOUS PARADIGM

Naomi didn't even like hearing her name spoken and said so. "Don't call me Naomi anymore," she said. Naomi was hurt, discouraged, and full of grief. She thought she had left Moab and its hurtful years behind, but in reality, she brought Moab with her to Bethlehem. Bethlehem had entered a new paradigm of prosperity and was nothing like Naomi remembered. Markets were busy, food was abundant, and everyone was happy — everyone except Naomi. Her point of reference went back 10 years to when Elimelech led her away from Bethlehem. She was mentally stuck in the previous paradigm of famine, only now its effect was compounded by the paradigm of loss she knew in Moab. Naomi's emotions were paralyzed and her hope was gone.

I trust I didn't just describe you. Perhaps everyone around you has moved on, but you can't seem to even take the smallest steps toward recovery. You dread that sermon the pastor brings every January from Philippians about "forgetting those things which are behind" (3:13). You don't say anything about it, but secretly, you're bothered by the cheerfulness of your neighbors and wonder, "Do they ever have a bad day?"

I learned years ago after experiencing a difficult disappointment that longing for what used to be cripples you from what is and handicaps you from what is to come. You must refuse to be buried in a grave of longing. I can't say anything is ever as simple as "just getting over it," because you will hurt and you will cry, but trying to find comfort within the city limits of misery will only delay your healing.

Continuing to hear people call her by the name, "Naomi," she stopped, turned to them, and demanded they never refer to her by that name again. Naomi said, "Call me 'Mara.'"

The name *Mara* means "bitter," and it perfectly described Naomi's feelings. You can find it in her own words as she remarked to her friends and said, "The Almighty has dealt bitterly with me" (Ruth 1:20).

How terribly sad someone's life could be so affected by such a negative paradigm that they would demand to be identified with it.

You know what? I can't find anywhere in the Book of Ruth that anyone referred to Naomi by the name Mara. It's not there. No one ever called her Mara, but continued to use the name they knew best, Naomi. As far as her friends and neighbors were concerned, she was still good and pleasant. The citizens of Bethlehem had come through a severe famine and knew God had been faithful to them. He would be to Naomi as well.

12

Paradigm Analysis

Self-diagnosis is at the very least risky, if not completely dangerous. There is never any balance in diagnosing your own problems, because you will either be too hard or too easy on yourself. It takes another set of eyes to see what you can't or won't see in yourself.

Paul addressed this in 2 Corinthians 10:12 when he wrote, "We dare not class ourselves or compare ourselves with those who commend themselves. But they, measuring themselves by themselves, and comparing themselves among themselves are not wise."

People on sinking ships cannot be helped by other people on higher decks of the same vessel. Salvation from disaster can come only from someone offering a lifeline extended from a different boat.

Naomi couldn't diagnose her condition as hard as she may have tried. If anything, she "misdiagnosed" herself on several counts. It took the neighbors and friends who managed to survive the famine in Bethlehem to analyze her problems and prescribe a remedy. They saw what

Naomi couldn't see and implemented strategies to help her recover and enjoy her life again.

The response of Naomi's Bethlehem friends reveals some valuable "paradigm principles" that if applied will help end paradigm paralysis and move you into your own new season of favor and blessing.

ENDING PARADIGM PARALYSIS

First, they did not allow Naomi's past paradigm of loss to determine her identity. Instead, the people of Bethlehem continued to call Naomi by her name, as if to say, "We know you've lost a husband, but 'you' are still Naomi." "We understand two sons have died and a daughter-in-law has walked away, but as for you, you're still Naomi."

You don't feel "good," but you are good; things don't appear to be pleasant, but your life will be marked by pleasant days again in the near future. The people of Bethlehem had moved into their new paradigm of God's visitation, and they would not allow one of their return-ing daughters to remain paralyzed by her past.

Circumstances must never define you. No amount of bad times must be allowed to remain attached to you with leech-like tentacles that mar your demeanor and outlook on life. You may have suffered a number of life's devastating setbacks, but those setbacks are not who you are. I purposed early in life that when I got into trouble, I would not let trouble get into me.

I've always appreciated what Paul said in 2 Corinthi-ans 4:8-9: "We are hard-pressed on every side, yet not crushed; we are perplexed, but not in despair; persecut-ed, but not forsaken; struck down, but not destroyed."

This comes from a man who bore the marks of beat-ings, shipwrecks, snakebite, and betrayal, but I can almost hear him say, "Don't judge me by what I've been through; mark me by what I've victoriously lived through." Paul would not be identified with anything except bearing the marks of Christ for the sake of the gospel. A man or woman, whose identity is secure in the relationship they have with Jesus, never needs to cower down to the ill-effects of difficult circumstances.

Second, Naomi's friends did not allow her circumstance to distort her view of God. I'm amazed when I read the few words that Naomi spoke on her return to Bethlehem.

Look carefully at four statements she makes:

(1) Naomi said to Ruth and Orpah in a conversation while in Moab, "The hand of the Lord is gone out against me."

(2) When returning to Bethlehem, Naomi said to her friends, "The Almighty has dealt very bitterly with me."

(3) Later she said, "I went out full, and the Lord has brought me home again empty."

(4) On a later occasion she said, "The Lord has testified against me, and the Almighty has afflicted me."

It's easy to get the impression she was blaming God for her troubles. Before you get too critical of Naomi, allow me to ask you a question: "What have you been through that may have altered and even distorted your view of God? Everything Naomi said was the result of a belief system that had been grossly affected by her troubles. Her view of a loving and compassionate God was now distorted, and she saw Him only as a severe judge meting out hard justice and punishment to those gone astray.

Job's wife must have felt the same way when she challenged her husband by saying, "Curse God and die." I've heard some really good sermons that take Job's wife to task. Some would preach about her lack of faith. Others would speak about what they considered to be her disrespect of God, as well as her husband. Some knowledgeable authors and speakers have referred to her as an accomplice of Satan. How could she have the audacity to suggest that her husband curse God and take his own life? I'll tell you how. Her troubles had altered her perspective.

She had lost the same home and security Job lost. No longer could she claim her place in society, but what's more important, her children, 10 of them, had been killed. Now she sits back and listens as Job's friends question her husband's integrity and challenge his faith in God.

With every recollection of those 10 children, the view of Job's wife was altered a little more. With every accusation of men who should know Job better than their accusations are reflecting, that perspective is affected again. It's entirely possible that when she couldn't take it anymore, she interrupted everything and indicated to Job it was time to drop the integrity thing and get life over with. Thus her plea: "Curse God and die" (Job 2:9).

As a church leader, I've often had women, similar to Job's wife, accompany their husbands to my office for counseling. As Pastor Job attempts to convince me he's "holding it together," Sister Job is holding back tears. Pastor Job is trying to appear strong in my presence, but Sister Job knows he was pacing the floor the night before, begging to die.

Maybe you're there. There was a time when you could never be accused of doubting or questioning God, but now, after the steady erosion of your confidence, you have to lay claim to a distorted view of Him.

What should you do?

A NEW PERSPECTIVE

You must gain a new perspective by climbing to a higher vantage point. God's promise to us found in

Isaiah 46:10 is that He makes known "the end from the beginning." How can that be? It's because from where He sits on His throne, God maintains a vantage point that allows Him to clearly see all things, and you are welcomed to ascend higher in your trust of Him. When you do, your view will readjust and your faith will once again be renewed.

Whatever the words of Job's wife did or didn't do for her husband, Job used them as a catalyst to regain his own determination.

Job refused to yield to his wife's distorted view, and in so many words said, "If I can curse God and die, then I can bless God and live."

A renewed view from a vantage point of faith goes a long way to cure a bad case of paradigm paralysis.

The third principle leading to Naomi's recovery is seen in how her friends refused to allow an old paradigm to devalue her potential.

By her own admission, Naomi returned to Bethlehem empty. In her estimation, she had nothing to show for the 10 years she had spent in Moab, but that's not entirely true. Actually, Naomi was burdened with more emotional baggage than she would ever be able to unpack. Naomi's speech revealed her bitterness, and some of her decisions displayed her hurt. Everywhere you look, it's easy to see the extreme cost of Naomi's 10-year journey. Yet, the fact she came back with someone of the character, integrity, and beauty of her daughter-in-law, Ruth, speaks volumes about the faint light of potential that still shined in Naomi's life.

You can't always help getting into trouble. Trouble comes to us because, according to the Bible, "It rains on the just and the unjust." You can count on it. It wasn't entirely Naomi's choice to go to Moab. She was taken there by a discouraged husband. While you can't always avoid getting into "Moab," you do have a say about what you take away.

"Stuff" will accumulate and attach itself as you journey through your own "Moab."

In Naomi's case, Orpah and Ruth attached themselves to her for a while. However, at the crossroads of choice and destiny, Naomi maintained the ability to allow the right one to leave and the right one to stay.

The Hebrew meaning of the name *Ruth* is "friend" and "vision of beauty." The Hebrew meaning of the name *Orpah* has to do with stubbornness and being stiff-necked. It's impressive that Naomi was able to see the difference between these two women. (I wonder if she worried about her son, Chilion, when he married her.)

Never forget that old paradigm—baggage is heavy and comes with the high price of stifling your future. Your future, however, can be rescued with one right decision of choosing beauty over stubbornness. In a "make-or-break" moment, Naomi separated from stubbornness and held tightly to something beautiful, and returned to Bethlehem, revealing the remnant of potential she still possessed.

NAOMI'S MESSIANIC DESTINY

The fourth principle demonstrated by the citizens of Bethlehem could have been the most important, because they refused to permit Naomi's circumstances to destroy her role in Messianic destiny.

The return of Naomi to Bethlehem was more about fulfilling a foreordained plan than it was repairing a past marked by failure and disappointment. God wanted Ruth in Bethlehem, and Naomi was the agent He used to get her there.

The beautiful story of Ruth culminates in her marriage to Boaz and the birth of the child named Obed. Ruth was the great-grandmother of David, whose throne and kingdom were established by God himself. The generations would pass until one day when Jesus would be known as the Son of David—by adoption through Joseph and by bloodline through Mary, both descendants of David. Naomi shared in that destiny because of her role in bringing Ruth to Bethlehem.

At Obed's birth, Naomi became caregiver to a child and, in essence, a dynasty, a generation that was prophetically aligned with the promises of the coming Messiah. How tragic it would have been if Naomi's destiny had been aborted before she came from Moab, but more so, had she arrived in Bethlehem only to have her destiny paralyzed by past grief.

The proclamation of Naomi's friends testifies of the unfolding plan of God in Naomi's life. Holding baby Obed in their arms, Naomi's friends enter her house with this declaration: "Blessed be the Lord, who has not left you this day without a near kinsman; and may his name be famous in Israel! And may he be to you a restorer of life and a nourisher of your old age; for your daughter-in-law . . . who is better to you than seven sons, has borne him" (Ruth 4:14-15).

The woman who earlier had confessed that life was over and little remained to live for, experienced a resurrection of purpose. Look at it: "Then Naomi took the child in her arms and cared for him. The neighbor women living there said, "Naomi has a son" (vv. 16-17).

In an instant, Naomi was translated into a paradigm of purpose. The moment Naomi embraced her calling, the rest of her life took on new meaning.

How about you?

Have you embraced your purpose or are you still tightly holding onto the memories of bitter history? You've hesitated to move into your future because of the loyalty you have to a former paradigm that doesn't exist anymore.

Your destiny is still in place. Occasionally, there will be detours and adjustments on the journey. Plans are sometimes altered, but purpose remains. You will arrive at your destined place, and the paradigm of continual joy and favor will be realized in your life.

13

More Than a Season

Iremember hearing the word "paradigm" for the first time as a young and eager pastor trying to get my bearings with a new congregation I had been assigned to in Texas. While attending a church growth seminar, I attentively listened as the instructor taught about "paradigm shifts." I'm embarrassed to admit my naivety, but while taking notes, I couldn't even spell the word, much less define its meaning. Another pastor sitting near me sensed my "greenness," and quipped about "pair of dimes" being equal to "twenty cents" and "pair-of-dime shifts" happen when two dimes are rubbed together. I returned his "class clown" humor with a slight grin, then again turned my attention to the speaker. In an hour's time, that instructor did more to help me understand my congregation and our mutual frustrations than I had been able to gain in the few months I had been their pastor. On that day, I discovered at least some of the "whys" behind the acceptance or the rejection most people have toward new methods and concepts. We are conditioned by the paradigms that help form us, and as a result, function accordingly.

By definition, a *paradigm* is a set of generally accepted assumptions or the vision of reality through which we perceive the world. It is a standard accepted by an individual or a society as a clear example, model, or pattern of how things should work. The term was brought to prominence by science-fiction writer and historian, Thomas Khun, in a book published in 1962, *The Structure of Scientific Revolution*. Khun defined *paradigms* as "the theoretical framework within which scientific thinking and practices operate." Since then, the term has been frequently associated with the understanding of world economies and politics, as well as social and religious practices. A "paradigm shift" describes the fundamental change of the usual and accepted way of thinking and performance in these and other areas of science, technology, and culture. In other words, it is a change in how one views the world.

Throughout history, various change agents have provoked and driven some paradigm shifts to happen so quickly that the world seemed to awaken one morning to find little was the same as the day before. For example, within a few hours of the horrific terrorist attack on America on September 11, 2001, new paradigms affecting everything from national security to global travel began to take form. Other examples include the effects of the ever-advancing breakthroughs in medicine, technology, and a myriad of scientific disciplines. For instance, try to imagine navigating through your day without Internet or cell phone capability. Everything from friendly email to top-level business transactions would be interrupted, if not jeopardized. Multiply that scenario exponentially as it relates to global governments and economies. Bottom line: Paradigms are both "effective" and "affective." They cause and create, and at the same time they influence and alter. One thing for sure—good or bad—they can last a long time.

EFFECTIVE AND INEFFECTIVE PARADIGMS

The Bible offers many examples of effective and ineffective paradigms. You can read about kingdoms rising or falling as a direct result of its embraced paradigm. I'll highlight a few of them for you.

King David's reign over the united kingdoms of Judah and Israel became the standard by which others would be judged in the future. His obvious and well-publicized faults notwithstanding, David was "a man after God's own heart" and established a paradigm of innovative leadership that led to kingdom consolidation and expansion. He prioritized worship and made the ark of the covenant and its return to Jerusalem his focused priority. The result was an unprecedented era of remarkable favor and blessings from the Lord.

Another example is King Josiah. Beginning at eight years of age, Josiah initiated a paradigm of righteous reform. He dismantled pagan altars and groves dedicated to idols. He renovated the Temple and rediscovered the Word of the Lord. Josiah led the kingdom of Judah through 31 years of revival, prompted by his emphasis on the Word of God.

By contrast, King Jeroboam led from a paradigm of evil, idolatry, and self-preservation. It was said he had "done more evil than any other king before him" (see 1 Kings 14:9). For 22 years, the nation of Israel suffered greatly and entered into an unusually long state of economic, social, and religious depression.

There were 42 different monarchs who reigned over Israel and Judah, and history hasn't been kind to most of them. Power does strange things to people who already have struggles with ego and pride. One of the strongest indictments made against any of Israel's leaders was with regard to King Saul. He had all the potential in the world, and could have brought Israel to its greatest days as its first-named king. Within days of his coronation, however, Saul began to function from a paradigm of uncertainty that became marked by his own suspicion, distrust, and jealousy of others. He was enslaved by his own need for control and openly displayed a horrific demeanor, marked by extreme paranoia.

It is discouraging to realize the failures of mortal men, the disappointing models of leadership, and the government some of them brought forth. Yet, the leaders who sought to know the Lord and follow after righteousness were able to inaugurate new paradigms of promise that prefigured the eternal reign of Christ and its blessed abundance.

A PARADIGM OF PEACE

One day while peering through the lens of prophetic inspiration, Isaiah foretold a paradigm of peace led by the Son of God. These words are wonderful to consider.

> For unto us a Child is born, unto us a Son is given; and the government will be upon his shoulder and His name will be called Wonderful, Counselor, Mighty God, Everlasting Father, Prince of Peace. Of the increase of His government and peace there will be no end" (Isaiah 9:6-7).

On another occasion, Isaiah prophesied to Israel of a great paradigm of increase and breakthrough that would surpass anything they had previously known.

> Do not remember the former things, nor consider the things of old. Behold, I will do a new thing, now it shall spring forth; Shall you not know it? I will even make a road in the wilderness and rivers in the desert. The beast of the field will honor Me, the jackals and the ostriches, because I give waters in the wilderness

and rivers in the desert, to give drink to My people,
My chosen. This people have I formed for Myself;
they shall declare My praise (Isaiah 43:18-21).

Other Old Testament prophets foretold extended seasons of grace, prosperity, and favor that would actually
evolve into paradigms of great blessing. From those paradigms, focused vision and godly wisdom would flow
from kingdom leaders, and the citizens beneath the um-
brella of their kingdom covering would reap the benefits
of its shelter.

Note the following examples:

- Haggai foretold a "glory" paradigm that would
  come with the building of the new temple (2:9).

- Joel prophesied of a paradigm of restoration accompanied by the outpouring of God's Spirit (2:28-32).

- Micah signaled the coming paradigm of the Messiah, pinpointing the town of the Lord's birth and
  likening His kingdom to a great mountain where
  people would find security and salvation (4:1-8).

- Zechariah proclaimed a paradigm of protection
  and intercession, when the office of priest and king
  would be brought together as one, and a person
  uniquely qualified would occupy both offices si-
  multaneously (6:13).

- Malachi heralded a paradigm of repentance and
  preparation for Israel in anticipation of a coming
  Messiah. Malachi even declared a "messenger of
  the covenant" would precede Him as a forerunner
  of this divine visitation (3:1).

These and other prophets served their generation
and spoke specifically to it. Often prophets would be
used of God to prophesy beyond the boundaries of
their generation into the lives of the nation's future
sons and daughters. Some of them never lived to see
their prophecies come to pass, but they died with great

comfort and confidence that the Word of God spoken through them would not return void, but would accomplish all God had designed.

THE PROMISES OF PARADIGMS TO COME

The promises of paradigms to come only intensify in the New Testament. In the fifth chapter of Matthew, Jesus spoke what became known as the Sermon on the Mount. He laid the foundation of a new paradigm of Kingdom living and Kingdom loving, unlike anything the world had known. Who among that mountainside audience would have dreamed that in the chaotic environment of a Roman-suppressed civilization, anything like Jesus was proposing in His sermon could be possible? Look at what He said:

Blessed are the poor in spirit, for theirs is the kingdom of heaven.

Blessed are those who mourn, for they shall be comforted.

Blessed are the meek, for they shall inherit the earth.

Blessed are those who hunger and thirst for righteousness, for they shall be filled.

Blessed are the merciful, for they shall obtain mercy.

Blessed are the pure in heart, for they shall see God.

Blessed are the peacemakers, for they shall be called sons of God.

Blessed are those who are persecuted for righteousness' sake, for theirs is the kingdom of heaven.

Blessed are you when they revile and persecute you, and say all kinds of evil against you falsely for My sake.

Rejoice, and be exceedingly glad: for great is your reward in heaven, for so they persecuted the prophets who were before you (Matthew 5:3-10).

With the Beatitudes, Jesus presented what a worldly system would define as a "paradigm of paradox" that doesn't resemble happiness. The Lord's message about true happiness doesn't fit the typical idea of getting all you can, having your own way, and climbing the ladder of success. Jesus knew the kind of happiness that can fill the void in every heart cannot be created by this world with its ideas of human satisfaction.

Hollow lives will never be filled by hollow things. Ask Solomon. He had everything a world of opulence could offer, but at the end of his life, Solomon summed up his overwhelming disappointments by saying, "Vanity of vanities, all is vanity" (Ecclesiastes 1:2). The truth is: physical things don't meet spiritual needs. Jesus summarized it best when He said, " One's life does not consist in the abundance of the things he possesses (Luke 12:15).

The kingdom of heaven models a different standard that defies worldly comprehension. In heaven's kingdom, the most exalted are those whom the world considers the least important. In heaven's kingdom, believers set their affections on things above rather than on things of earth. In heaven's kingdom, its citizens understand the first shall be last and the last shall be first. In the kingdom of heaven, the way up is down. In heaven's kingdom, those who lead understand they must lead like Jesus and be the servant of all (see Luke 22:26).

A MILLENNIAL PARADIGM

Try to imagine a nation where Jesus is the president or an earthly kingdom where Christ is king. Every scriptural example of a goodly and godly dominion points to the time when that hope becomes reality.

One of the earliest promises of such an awesome age can be found in Psalm 2:6-8:

Yet I have set My King on my holy hill of Zion.

I will declare the decree: The Lord has said to Me,

You are My Son, Today I have begotten You.
Ask of Me, and I will give You
The nations for Your inheritance,
And the ends of the earth for Your possession.

One of the most beautiful descriptions of a Christ-ruled kingdom is found in Isaiah 11:1-9.

> There shall come forth a Rod from the stem of Jesse, and a Branch will grow out of his roots. The Spirit of the Lord shall rest upon Him, and the Spirit of wisdom and understanding, the Spirit of counsel and might, the Spirit of knowledge and of the fear of the Lord. His delight is in the fear of the Lord, and He shall not judge by the sight of His eyes, nor decide by the hearing of His ears; but with righteousness He shall judge the poor, and decide with equity for the meek of the earth; He shall strike the earth with the rod of His mouth, and with the breath of His lips He shall slay the wicked. Righteousness shall be the belt of His loins, and faithfulness the belt of His waist. The wolf also shall dwell with the lamb, the leopard shall lie down with the young goat, the calf and the young lion and the fatling together; and a little child shall lead them. The cow and the bear shall graze; their young ones shall lie down together; and the lion shall eat straw like the ox. The nursing child shall play by the cobra's hole, and the weaned child shall put his hand in the viper's den. They shall not hurt nor destroy in all My holy mountain, for the earth shall be full of the knowledge of the Lord, as the waters cover the sea.

John, in Revelation, describes this age as nothing short of heaven on Earth where Satan is bound, saints are free, sickness is gone, and joy never ends.

Then I saw an angel coming down from heaven, having the key to the bottomless pit and a great chain in his hand. He laid hold of the dragon, that serpent of old, who is the Devil and Satan, and bound him for a thousand years; and he cast him into the bottomless pit, and shut him up, and set a seal on him, so that he should deceive the nations no more till the thousand years were finished (20: 1-3a).

Blessed and holy is he who has part in the first resurrection. Over such the second death has no power, but they shall be priests of God and of Christ, and shall reign with Him a thousand years (20:6).

What a wonderful and glorious future awaits those who serve the Lord. The blessings that accompany the Amos 9:13 promises are simply a thrilling and prefiguring type of the unending and magnificent age to come.

The promises of Amos 9:13 are more than seasonal manifestations.

Much more.

EPILOGUE

Amos was an eighth-century prophet from Judah who performed his prophetic ministry in Israel. It is likely he traveled from his hometown in Tekoa, about 10 miles south of Bethlehem, to Israel's capital city for only a short time—perhaps just a matter of days—delivered his heart-searing message and returned home We're not even sure how effective his ministry was in his own time.

He temporarily left the solitary life of a shepherd and daringly proclaimed God's strong Word in the shadow of the false temple in Bethel. His prophecy condemned social injustice, moral degeneracy, and backsliding.

However, in the midst of a scorching message of condemnation and a call for God's justice to roll down like mighty waters, Amos declared the possibility of an unusual intervention of God: if God's people would receive and cherish the revelation He granted them and respond with obedience and faithfulness, a time of incredible blessing would break forth. "Things are going to happen so fast your head will swim, one thing fast in the heels of the other. You won't be able to keep up. Everything will be happening at once-and everywhere you look, blessings! Blessings like wine pouring off the mountains and hills" (Amos 9:13 MSG)

We are living in that Amos 9:13 season. We are living in the speed of favor.

Thank God for the favor, for the "everywhere you look, blessings!"

At the same time, we must make sure to understand the parameters of God's favor.

Favor does not mean nothing ever goes wrong. We are highly favored, but we still get wet when it rains. We're blessed, but sometimes the car needs new tires. We're chosen, but sometimes the kids need braces. We're elected, but sometimes we're selected to endure a test. We don't always get the parking place nearest the mall entrance. We don't get an upgrade to first class on every flight. Favor is not fantasy.

I've laughed at the story of the pastor who was attempting to lose weight and told his staff he would not stop at the Krispy Kreme doughnut shop unless God provided a parking space right in front. When he showed up at the office with a box of doughnuts, they observed that God must have been gracious and arranged for the parking space. He responded, "Well, He did. He didn't do it right away, but by the time I circled the block six times, He arranged it."

Despite what you may hear from some, God's favor doesn't always ensure you will live without challenges and everything will always go your way. His favor is grace. We live by grace.

In the Amos paradigm, favor has a divine origin that no man can produce, but provides opportunities that an obedient heart positions him to receive. In the Amos paradigm, the favor of God isn't only about overcoming negative circumstances; it's also about taking advantage of them and realizing that somehow, God did for you what you couldn't do for yourself.

That was true of Joseph who was elevated from prisoner to prime minister, because he found favor with the Pharaoh.

It was true of Noah who saved his family from the Flood, because he found favor (grace) in the eyes of the Lord.

The same was true of Esther who saved a nation by finding favor with the king.

It was true for Paul who endured the suffering of storms and snakebite more than can possibly be imagined.

Paul's trials are astounding to consider . . .

- Three different times, he was beaten with rods.
- He was involved in three horrifying shipwrecks.
- Paul spent an entire day and night treading water in the deep ocean.
- He was mauled by wild beasts and betrayed by some he had once trusted.

On top of all of these things, Paul said in First Corinthians 15:31, "I face death on a daily basis."

Some would consider these things as a blatant attack of Satan to destroy Paul. Indeed, the Apostle was targeted for destruction. But take note of what was written by Paul in 1 Corinthians 15:10: "Whatever I am now, it is because God poured out his special favor on me—and not without results. For I have worked harder than any of the other apostles; yet it was not I but God who was working through me by His grace" (NLT).

How could Paul in any way link his trials to the favor of God?

Paul realized that everything he had faced had been used by God to spread the gospel of Jesus. His thoughts are revealed in Philippians 1:12: "I want you to know brothers that the things that have happened to me have actually turned out for the furtherance of the gospel."

And so it is that in the Amos paradigm that problems become possibilities, obstacles become opportunities, and troubles become triumphs.

Yes, we are living in grace. Our lives move at the speed of favor—God's favor.

It is a favor that defines this very special season, and yes, even a paradigm of unprecedented blessings where God will:

- Exceed all we expect
- Increase all we invest
- Accelerate time to fulfill His kingdom purpose in us.